A revolutionary concept: church is either a daring adventure or nothing at all! From someone who has been in the trenches in every   hurch, Doug presents a profoundly simple strategy—don't sett^   ^r of the month, but allow the Lord to "loose" your ^   it go."

> —Dr. Jay Stra~~ck~~
> CEO/Presi~~dent~~
> Student Lea~~dership~~

I have had the privilege to walk with Dr. Dees for nine years. I have watched Doug work with staff to create new, innovative ways to help our church grow. His book has blessed me and I encourage you to allow the principles he teaches assist you in being more successful in our Lord's Kingdom work.

> —Pastor Randall James
> Chairman of the Southern Baptist Convention's
> Executive Committee
> First Orlando Foundation, President

reSymbol *will help you to become a winner in life and your church. I highly recommend that you ask yourself the tough questions Doug suggests. Life is too short to not move forward.*

> Pat Williams
> Senior Vice President, Orlando Magic
> Author of 'Extreme Dreams Depend on Teams'

reSymbol *provides a much-needed "head jerk" for today's church leaders. With powerful insight and exhortation, Doug Dees redirects our efforts, our passion and our process for effective church ministry. Read it and reap the rewards.*

> —Dr. David Ferguson,
> Intimate Life Ministries and the Great
> Commandment Network

reSymbol

A Guide to reThink, reDefine,
and reLease the Church

reSymbol

A Guide to reThink, reDefine, and reLease the Church

DOUG DEES

HigherLife
DEVELOPMENT SERVICES
Orlando, Florida

reSymbol
by Doug Dees

Published by HigherLife Development Services, Inc.
2342 Westminster Terrace
Oviedo, Florida 32765
407-563-4806
www.ahigherlife.com

ISBN: 978-1-935245-11-7
ISBN:1-935245-11-7

Cover Design: Kendal Alexander Media Operations
Author Photo by Dale Stroud www.MissionFieldImages.com

First Edition
09 10 11 12 13 – 5 4 3 2 1
Printed in the United States of America

Thank You

I wear two rings.

On my left hand is the one that says I am married to an incredible woman. Karen—thank you for walking alongside this right-brained guy. You are a great wife and an amazing mom—I love you! and thank you for loving me!

On my right hand I wear a ring which has three Greek words on it. Translated they say, "I am not my own." Jesus—I am Yours. Thank You so much for allowing me to be a part of Your kingdom and to work on Your behalf among your people. It is an honor that You know I cannot even begin to explain!

So, I am married to two people. I have "hers and his" rings. Without His provision for both my wife and His salvation, I would just be wasting oxygen and dating the planet looking for Karen.

I would also like to thank my two adult kiddos, Katie and Matt, for putting up with me while it looked like I was going through a "midlife crisis." It is actually just a "God-life crisis."

Thank you to DB2, my Dream Builders Network group, who has supported me as we all dream great things for God. Thank you Marvin and Mark for stepping up financially to help me launch ReleasingChurches.org. You truly are what friends look like.

And thank you to Dave Welday and the incredible team at HigherLife Development for taking on this odd project and believing in me enough to push it through.

God, take this and use it to Your glory!

Table of Contents

Introduction

WE ALL KNOW SOMETHING is wrong. Deep in our souls we are longing for anything that will make church seem more—well—real. You may have grown up in church, or are a leader in a church, or maybe you have never been around a church. In any case, each of you probably senses something has got to change. There is something missing. And we must find it.

I grew up around church. I think what has happened is this. Those of us who know church are doing the last things we were told to do. And we have forgotten why. It seems like what we do just doesn't seem to really matter anymore. There seems to be very little impact. In fact there seems to be more churches dying than living. And yet here we are, going through the motions like spiritual mimes. Not sure what to do to change it all. Not all churches suffer from this. But I'll bet you know one.

I for one am tired of keeping the system going. My "church arms" are exhausted. I'm so ready to change what I do and how I do it. I am willing to rethink everything in order to line up with what I sense the Father is saying to me.

He knows what is missing. He knows how we got here. He is dying to see us change. After all, we are His Son's bride.

If you want your life to matter, and you want church to matter, maybe you can help us reSymbol this system into something with life that changes lives. It may not be easy, but I think it is the only option we have. I cannot wait to see what He does.

. . . from visual to visible.

This book is for individuals and church leadership teams who want change for the better. So read it on two levels. First, by asking yourself this question: Can I change? And next: Can I help our church change?

We need change—not to use someone else's slogan. For too long in the West we've spent much of our time on the visuals—buildings, budgets, events, print media, and websites. Those are fine unless they become the major focus of our time and money. As I understand God and what He wrote, we are to make Christ "visible" to those whom we meet and to those whom we walk with on the journey. We need new visible symbols of success.

I'm not an expert on this. I have made as many mistakes as I have had successes over the past 19 years. Most of the successes, I stumbled upon. If not for God's grace I would not even be in His kingdom work. I have just found some things that make sense, and I thought I would write them down.

The chapters are not all the same length because they each have differing intents. Some have diagrams. Some do not. And the first two chapters are out of order on purpose. If this bothers you, you may not want to read any further. If, however, you can get past this, then I'll bet you can reSymbol.

Much of what is discussed is in the form of questions. The intent is to rattle your mind, to inspire your brain to start thinking of different actions than it has in the past. This book is somewhat of a primer; it depends on where you are as to how tough the book is to read.

I want to cause your default setting to be altared (not altered).

This does not mean that actions are the most important parts of faith. Faith without actions is dead. But actions without faith are built upon mankind. The church is not to be built upon mankind. So at the outset I want to say that you must be asking our Lord to open your mind to rethinking some things. We have built church on our desires for too long. Let's ask Him how He may want us to reSymbol it.

Chapter 2
Defining Visuals

Yes, we are starting with chapter two. Chapter one was just too depressing to start the book. The fact that something I love so much is in such disrepair breaks my heart. There are days I feel like Nehemiah when he heard that the walls of Jerusalem, the much loved "city of God," were torn down. The church of the west is in trouble in some spots. Many spots. But we will get to that in the next chapter. From the times of the early church until now we have had visual symbols define who we are. The Encarta encyclopedia defines a symbol as: "something that stands for or represents something else—especially an object representing an abstraction."

INDIVIDUALLY

In each chapter I want to start with a paragraph of thoughts for each of us as a person. One individual who is a part of the whole. But a part which must change before he or she can even think about affecting change in the larger system. As you read this chapter, think about what visuals you have as default settings in your mind. You assume it has always been that way. It hasn't. What things have you taken for granted and you have no idea why you do what you do. It is just the way it has been. What things (visuals) do you know to have some meaning to the members, but you wonder what they mean to others? To those outside the church, what do you think they mean?

Those who do not believe in this Christ we follow often think that all we do is about a place. A place called "church." They do not know that our God wants to be worshiped in spirit and in truth. They see bricks and mortar, even though we really worship in abstract. So how abstract is your church? What do people really see when they look at your places of gathering? Should that be their focus? How can we redirect their lines of sight so that the abstraction (Christ) is completely clear? Do the symbols represent anything anymore that has substance? I am not saying they don't. We had just better rethink it and make sure they DO represent Him and Him alone. As Christians who meet at church, what are we really about? Do we explain our symbols in such a way that people can truly know Him?

What if all these symbols were actually getting in the way of the gospel of Christ? Wouldn't we want to make sure we are not blocking someone's view of Christ?

There are many symbols. Like the fish (one of the oldest symbols), cathedrals, the huge Celtic crosses (many of the Island of Iona), and works of art. You can go visit the symbols of the past. The cathedrals of Europe are beautiful. Empty, but beautiful. Symbols are items or places that represent what we do and who we are. Some symbols are coming back into vogue. Celtic crosses are being used more. Even though no one is really sure what the circle around the middle of the cross represents, we use them today. We still use the fish. We have also added a few—the steeple, the building, the old church bell, and in more modern times, our logo or brand.

Symbols aren't bad. But they have the possibility of hindering the visibles He intended. People outside the church would most likely recognize these visuals as our symbols. But what do they represent? What comes to the mind of someone who does not know Christ? Is it abstract or clear? Within the church, we have symbols too—the budgets, buildings, baptism, bible study numbers, the programs, the bulletin, and styles of worship. Many of these symbols we use not only define ourselves but also are visual symbols of success and measurements of growth. They have taken on a life of their own. The visuals have, in some ways, become so heightened that Christ seems barely visible.

The metaphor has become the message. We have to take it backwards.

Wouldn't we want to make sure we are not blocking someone's view of Christ?

WE MUST MOVE FROM VISUAL TO VISIBLE

What are the symbols of Christ's church in the future? The early church had its visual symbols. But that is not how it started. The church of the future will focus more on the new symbols, which are actually very old—Christ's character, His attributes and His qualities. This is an abstraction as the definition defines. Abstract is hard to explain, but you know it when you see it. It has qualities beyond measurement. These qualities are evident when we see someone loving others. They are visible, but have no corresponding visuals. For example, what visual comes to mind when you think of this word—patience? It is hard to conjure up a picture in your mind. If something did come to mind, it is more likely a person from your past who exhibited patience toward you.

So the answer to the first question of reSymbol: Who do you want to look like? is Christ, of course. God can change a person's character to the image of Christ, but can He change a declining church in the same way?

Is character important enough for us to make it the central focus of the Christian life and of a local church? It is what God intended—that we become more like Jesus as we are conformed to His image (Romans 8:29). If He desires it of us individually, doesn't He also desire that when we group together?

Much of what He wants to do is not as controllable as we would like it to be. Releasing is just not that measurable. I am not saying we shouldn't measure or count or score. Just be careful. In the Old Testament, David found out how costly it was to count (1 Chronicles 21), when, even though he was in charge of everything, he wanted a census to find out just how much he was in control of. He pursued numbers. It backfired. Could it be that what you have is slipping away because you are counting too much and holding too tightly? Thinking it is all about us and our accomplishments or potential accomplishments? Not that we should not know WHO is there, but we seem to be consumed with how many. At times we may have sinned in God's eyes by measuring what we have instead of pursuing and releasing what He wants.

We are at a major ecclesiastical crossroad. Ask yourself this question: How effective will the symbols of success of the past be during the next twenty years? As the "church-planting movement" and the "emergent church movement" hit hard in the west, what will the landscape look like in two decades? What visuals will remain? What visible attributes will take hold?

BRANDING

In the Wild West it was about knowing which steer belonged to which rancher. We have my grandfather's branding iron. It has a mixture of the letters G L C. That stood for George Lewis Cozby. Every cow he owned had his brand. And everyone around there knew who GLC was. Bud. Bud Cozby. He had a farm for many years outside of Crowley, Texas. So his symbol had meaning. Everybody knew what a brand was, and everybody knew whose brand was whose.

Branding is still used on ranches. Some use chips. There is a large argument about microchip branding. It sounds like the government wants to microchip all the animals for control and counting purposes. Some ranchers are resisting.

It sounds similar to the same argument of King David's time.

> God can change a person's character to the image of Christ, but can He change a declining church in the same way?

In our visual world, the word branding is used in the advertising/marketing realm to describe how we define who we are and how people view us. It is a process which takes you through some tough thinking. Who do we think we are? Who do we want others to think we are? Who are we really? How do we portray that to them through words, deeds, and visuals?

The church may need to quit spending so much time and money on the visual side of branding and more time on rebranding the character side of visible. That will make more sense later on.

The early church had a brand—love—as deeds based on the love of God and others. The world of Rome knew of the disciples and of Him, and what they stood for (John 13:35). Our brand in many churches these days is one of dead visuals. We need a shift. A rebranding.

HOW DO WE SHIFT?

At first glance on paper, moving from visual to visible seems to be an easy thing. Within denominations and within each church there usually are some theological agreements. And you can depend on unity on a few basic tenets. But when you start messing with methodology—the "how you do things"—it is as if you have thrown your theology out the window. The word castigation comes to mind. Not pretty. There are so many unwritten rules of engagement that our correct theology is worthless. We have bylaws that we believe are true. We have documents which contain our vision statement, our mission statement, and our business practices. We have a two-inch thick, three-ring binder which holds the operations manual. All of these may be true and right. We also have the Bible in print. When the aforementioned documents supersede the Bible, we are done.

We follow what WE have put in print and disregard what HE has put in print.

We spend an inordinate amount of time designing ways of processing people, so that when we are done with them they are what we intended. To carry out all that we have put in print, we must have processes and procedures. We then take those and design a time in which we do those. That would be Sunday morning. We then decide what space is needed to accomplish the aforementioned lists and tasks. We then move toward designing the manufacturing areas (buildings) for our processes and systems to function.

We then need to secure the raw materials—people. So, we put what people we have to getting more people into the process. This often seems to lend itself to process over people. We have done all that we have put in print. But in the process, very few people feel loved (what He asked us to do), and few disciples ever emerge out of the process (another thing He asked us to do). Right now you are either agreeing with me or mad at me. Either way, ask yourself this question: When was the last time someone told you they wanted to be processed? Or assimilated? We may say our processes are for people. But people want something different than what most of us are offering. They might even want what God is asking us to give them in the first place. They want to be loved and accepted; they want help to know how to live life. I am not going to quote the studies here or do another one. We have read them and in our hearts we already know what we should be offering the planet. He told us what to offer the planet…HIM! I wonder how God feels about all this. I think it breaks the heart of Jesus when we put all that we do before the people He died for.

> The church may need to quit spending so much time and money on the visual side of branding and more time on rebranding the character side of visible.

We have to shift. In a later chapter we'll discuss just how to make this shift without everybody getting thrown from the bus. Our shift may come with great peril, but there is no option. It is time. Martin Luther knew well how much he was giving up and he gave it up anyway.

THE END RESULT

You have heard it said, begin with the end in mind. So, just where do we want to end up once we have "reSymboled"? It is not a destination. It is a way of life. Part of our problem is that we have viewed "church" as a destination and not a way of life. If reSymboled, then life in Christ (or church) is more of a "way" to be and less of a "place" to go. If our desired end result is attendance, then we take one path. If our desired end result is property, then we take another particular path. If our end results are programs, or parishioners, or events, we take yet other paths. But if our desired end result is to be disciples, we need to quit taking paths and take a look at some questions and motives. Questions like these: Will this path take us to where we want to go? What symbols are important and which ones are not, if we are to be discipling?

When was the last time someone told you they wanted to be processed?

First, we need to know where we are in the process so we can leave that place and go to another.

DISCUSSION GROUP

I suggest you find two or more friends and discuss what you have read. The best way I believe to do that is for each of you to go back and highlight the five questions or statements that God used to impact you in this last chapter. Then get together, order takeout, and sit and talk about why those words struck you and how God may be using them in your life.

You will see this same paragraph at the end of each chapter, because I think it is important to talk to others about what God is doing.

Chapter 1

The Idol Movement

A ND NOW FOR CHAPTER one. The "western church" is not to be confused with the "cowboy church," which has a western flair. It's about what you probably already know, but don't want to admit. Church in America is sick. Not dead as some say, but sick. Whether you are a part of a congregation that is 130 years old or 13 years old—for many of you— where you are in church life is not where you want to be. You can pick up a book by Barna Research Group* or LifeWay® Research** to get all the facts and figures you want. I will not go into them here. It is enough to say this: We believers in

---

* According to its website, "Barna Group is a visionary research and resource company located in Ventura, California. The firm is widely considered to be the leading research organization focused on the inter- section of faith and culture." (http://www.barna.org/about)

** According to its website, "LifeWay® Christian Resources of the Southern Baptist Convention is one of the world's largest providers of Christian products and services, including Bibles, church litera- ture, books, music, audio and video recordings, church supplies, and Internet services through LifeWay.com." (http://www.lifeway.com/lwc/ mainpage/0,1701,M%253D200724,00.html)

the west have it as good as it has ever been in Christendom, and we are not getting the job done.

NOTE: To church planters. You may want to skip this chapter since you are leading a new church. However, you may NEED to read this chapter to avoid being here yourself real soon!

A FEW OBSERVATIONS

Maybe you've said this: "There used to be growth and a vibrant atmosphere when we gathered, or at least some calm comfort spot we called 'church.' Now there seems to be less people in some of those spots—most of those spots. What to do?"

There are more variations of these comfort spots than anyone could have ever imagined. An attempt to define their distinctives and categorize them is like thinking that your new computer will be the standard for longer than one month. So I am not going to even try.

However, we can describe the state of the church by looking at characteristics of its behavior. Many churches have similar symptoms. Many of these observations cross old denominational lines. Like Marble Slab Creamery® ice cream, there is a blending that makes each church unique, but can also make its sickness and possible death unique. Can we help expose even more the uniqueness symptom, cure it, and expose Christ in the middle of each group of believers?

We must take into consideration a few things about where we all are (in no special order):

- Some are committed to Christ and His church, just not to the organization called "church."
- There seems to be a desire among some believers to live like missionaries in their own towns.
- Some established churches have a commitment to "church, then Christ," others, "Christ, then church."
- Some have a commitment to Christ "outside" the system called "church."
- Some desire to stay fixed to the programs, buildings, and methods of the past—their symbols.
- There is a nomadic (seemingly noncommittal) nature of many next-generation Christians. Is this a new symbol?
- Some desire to broaden the scope and ways we do what we do with different symbols.
- Some want to invite those who do not know Christ to a building they call "the church."
- There seems to be an entrepreneurial wind blowing. There may be many failed attempts, but they keep trying.
- There are planting movements across our planet whose viral nature defies explanation.

On the one hand, we have a desire to reach beyond where we have been in the past and in ways that are not proven, to step out on faith. On the other hand, we have the established church, which is still somewhat effective in some areas, but not as effective in exponential ways that it probably could be. Can the two come together? Should they?

THE REMNANT

Can we find the remnant in each established church that is willing to reach beyond their walls to those around them, and at the same time hand the church off to the next generation? Can we find ways to empower them to take the church to the world daily, instead of waiting until Sunday? And will the next generation even want that church?

Many churches are in decline. Depending on who you read, there are approximately 400,000 churches in America. I wonder how many of those churches will be in existence in 10 years? I am not saying this because I think they are doing a bad job at being Christians or "doing church."

I don't believe that these churches are full of people who don't care. They are just not sure what the next right thing to do is. I believe these churches are worth saving.

Society has just changed and is changing rapidly. Due to the Internet's mass pollination of ideas and thoughts, all areas of America—metro, rural, and isolated—are a few years into some major changes. Are these churches ready and willing to change the delivery system of Christ to make it match what the world is asking for?

About 70% of churches have reached a plateau, or are in decline, in terms of growth. You will get a slightly different number than this depending on who you talk to. But the number will probably be higher. However, the emergent church movement and the church planting movement will potentially surpass the current church numbers in the next few years. Why? Because it seems that the emerging and newly planted churches are more successful at intentionally interacting with today's culture. More established churches have a disadvantage here. But they cannot avoid the fact that they must figure out HOW to interact with their culture.

I don't believe that these churches are full of people who don't care. They are just not sure what the next right thing to do is.

Of the 44,000 Southern Baptist churches in America, 34,000 or so are plateaued or declining. Dr. Frank Page, President of the Southern Baptist Convention at the time of this statement, said in June of 2008 that unless the church changes its methodology, more than half of the Southern Baptist churches will disappear in the near future. "If we don't start paying attention to the realities...by the year 2030, we will be proud to have 20,000 rather than 44,000 Southern Baptist churches. We are a generation of old white folks trying to hold on till we die." In order to avoid a decline, Page recommends that the church reach out to ethnic minorities and young people.*

Dr. Page is right. We all must reach out to those who do not know Christ. Young people, minorities, whoever you meet today! In Orlando there are no majorities, only minorities. There is not one ethnic group which has enough to be considered a majority. And we have snowbirds who are here half of the year, and retirees who stay here. We also have 62% of the adult population which is single.

Within the Central Florida area we have the whole planet. One study showed we have 147 languages spoken in the Central Florida school system.** In fact, according to Mark Weible, Greater Orlando Baptist Association (GOBA) Church Planting Specialist, the total attendance of GOBA's 160 churches did not increase from 1990–2000. During this same eight-year period, this geographical area grew in population by 45%. In Florida as a whole, more than 2,100 Baptist churches are flat and declining.*** This is not meant to shed any negative light on the administration over these churches. With all these people and all these types, what is the problem? This is a target-rich environment. But are you shooting at a target that no longer exists?

It is simply this. The environment in which these churches were initially planted no longer exists.

---

* Bob Smietana, "Leader Says Southern Baptists Must Change," *The Tennessean*, Sunday, 1 June 2008.

** http://www.puertorico-herald.org/issues/2002/vol6n19/Schools2WaySt-en.html

*** Mark Weible, conversation with author, Orlando, FL, May 2008

Here is a shameless plug for my nonprofit group. I have started a new ministry, ReleasingChurches.org, a 501c3 nonprofit consulting group. The churches we have the potential to help are those churches in the 70%(ish), who agree they need help and are willing to change. Initial promotion will be conducted in partnership with GOBA Executive Director of Missions, Dr. Bill Faulkner, beginning fall of 2009. We plan to "focus group" the new materials then beta test them with the entire association. These materials will redirect focus to each congregant and their daily lives as well as their collective gatherings in worship and bible study.

But are you shooting at a target that no longer exists?

Funding partners are needed during the first two years. We already have plans to attend meetings of Metro education pastors as well as seek out other potential clients. We intend to utilize the positive results within GOBA to fan the flames of potential change elsewhere. I need your help to begin this process. A prospectus/business plan is available upon request at www.ReleasingChurches.org. Thanks!

BACK TO THE STORY

Many people these days seem to say, "Jesus sounds pretty good to me, but I can hardly stand His fiancée." The bride of Christ is sometimes unappealing and appalling in the way she treats those whom He died for. If Jesus and His bride were a couple, would you invite them to dinner? I am not railing on the bride. I am railing on us as leaders. It is our fault. We made her the way she is. The way WE are. This bride is so programmed and structured that she has no personality, no character. She is just duty and obedience. She is complacency with no depth. If you have ever seen the original 1975 *Stepford Wives*, you get the picture. She is the word love with no meaning behind it. So why don't we just call her what she is and move on to plant new churches? Why? Because He died for her. We cannot throw out the churches of the past. We who lead must allow ourselves to be used by God to help change her into the bride He is waiting to meet. We must learn to have symbols that are visible without becoming stagnant visuals.

You must first decide "who" or "what" you want to look like before you can assign "how" you will do what it takes. Do you want to look like other Christians or more like Christ? Can you do both? Do you want your church to look like other churches or like what Christ wants it to look like? Can it do both? We have figured out how to drum up attendance but have forgotten how to disciple and reproduce people who look like Christ. At least in the ways Christ did in Luke 10.

THE DILEMMA OF THE "ESTABLISHED CHURCH"

Within each church I hope there is a remnant. But much of the time that remnant is encased by the establishment. The word established used to be a good thing. Now it may not be so. It is cool to have "Est. 1803" as a part of your advertising campaign if you are selling cooking flour. If, however, "Est." means stuck and not moving forward, you most likely will not exist in 20 years—no matter the fact that you have existed for over one hundred years. Even though you may have some guests come through the front door.

"Jesus sounds pretty good to me, but I can hardly stand His fiancée."

Questions the established church must seriously ask itself:

- Can we reach beyond our walls using the "symbols" of our recent past?
- If we want to reach people for Christ, are we willing to redefine a lot of what we do?
- Can we do less policing and more releasing?
- Are we willing to find out what that means for us?
- Are we willing to rethink what success is?
- Can we refocus our theology?
- Can we redefine our ideology?
- Will we redefine our words?
- Can we stop using parts of a system which worked at one time but is not working now?
- Are we using people to build a church or a church to build people?

- Are we willing to redefine what works?
- Is it more important to us that Christ be known than to have our preference in church structure?
- Are we willing to reSymbol?

If you feel you are ready to rethink your symbols, we will start asking some tough questions. Questions which, if you are honest, will expose answers that will help you move toward God's dream for you and your church. Are you willing to "reSymbol" in order to "resemble" Christ more? There is no shame in saying no. Be honest. Become aware of your own thoughts, feelings, and fears. Spend time talking to God about it. Let Him tell you how He wants to go about forming you and your church into the image of His Son. Don't let a book force it on you. Let Him walk you through it in His ways and His timing.

THE EMERGENT CHURCH

I cannot find a decent definition which does not have a slam against it in the middle or a case for it at the end. So I will make up my own. Here it is—"Emergent church: the church that is emerging."

The good news of Jesus is being spread thickly across our world.

How easy was that? There is a church that is emerging. It seems to be those below the age of 35-40. As I read their websites, it seems to me that there are probably three camps. Those who have ditched theology and methodology; those who have kept their theology but ditched the methodology; and those who are trying to figure out which group they want to be.

The established church seems to look on with disdain at all three groups. My times sitting with their leaders tells me that the second group (those who have kept their theology and ditched the methodology) have a lot to offer. They seem to understand and are very committed to the biblical text and Jesus as a loving Lord and Savior. They have just seen that the methodology of the past no longer works in reaching people for Christ and letting them know who He is and that He loves them. After all, they say, isn't that the purpose of church? Isn't that what He asked us to do, to love God and love others?

So if you are in an established church, before you throw rocks at the emergent group, sit down and have a genuine conversation about what they believe. If you are in the emergent group, you need to do the same with the established church. Take time to Google: "Ed Stetzer and the emerging church."

THE CHURCH PLANTING MOVEMENT

It is happening overseas. It's viral and America may have the bug. In the past four years at FBC Orlando (First

Baptist Church of Orlando) there has been an event called National New Church Conference (also called Exponential Conference). It is the largest gathering of church planters in America. Here is the blurb for Tim Keller, one of the keynote speakers, from the 2009 Exponential Conference website:

> Tim Keller is the founding and lead pastor of Redeemer Presbyterian (PCA), "one of Manhattan's most vital congregations," according to *Christianity Today* [12/04]. Redeemer Presbyterian Church started a Church Planting Center in 2001, and its phone has not stopped ringing since. He is committed to the church planting movement and entering the culture's stories and retelling them with the gospel. Redeemer's vision is to spread the gospel; first through ourselves and then through the city by word, deed, and community. To bring about personal changes, social healing, and cultural renewal through a movement of churches and ministries that change New York City, and through it, the world." Keller promotes piety, evangelistic outreach, and missions of mercy. His recent books include: *The Reason for God* (Feb 2008) and *The Prodigal God* (Oct 2008). Tim will be presenting special insights via video.

Does that verbiage sound like your church?

But can the established church be a better version of themselves?

The growth of the Exponential Conference over the past four years has been, well, exponential! Planters are planting in unbelievable ways. The seeds of Christ are being sown in ways none of us could have imagined 20 years ago. The good news of Jesus is being spread thickly across our world and people are coming to Christ as their Savior. Though this movement is happening at light speed, there are many churches that do not see it or feel it. The established church may want to jump in but just doesn't know how. They know they can't be just like some of the other churches, which are more emergent and have a planter's entrepreneurial spirit. But why should they have to?*

Some are throwing gas on the fire.

These are just a few examples. There is so much new happening in the kingdom it is impossible to list.

Vision360—Al Weiss, President of Disney, wants to plant 1,000 churches. Steve Johnson, the President of Vision360 is a friend of mine. They are serious about this.**

Northwood Church—Bob Roberts. Bob joined with Al Weiss to be a part of VisionUSA. The name changed to Vision360. Bob and Northwood in Keller, Texas had already planted about 90+ churches before partnering with Vision360. They are still going.

VisionNationals—Arjuna Chiguluri of India. In an email on 3/15/09, Arjuna wrote: "VN has started over 300 churches in India. Most of them, probably about 200 out of

---

* See: www.ExponentialConference.org.

** See: www.Vision360.org.

the 300, do not have buildings. Apart from church services these places are being used for Wednesday and Friday fasting prayers and also some believers will go to the church in a particular time to pray and intercede. Also used for the functions of church believers. The church building in Vizag was used also for a school until we ran out of space."*

CMAResources.org—Neil Cole. Neil helps churches understand organic growth. They are making a huge impact at an incredible rate.

These are not meant to sound trite or to put you to shame. But we have to get EVERYBODY OUT OF THE STANDS AND INTO THE GAME! These ministries are only a few of those attempting to do so.

I am so glad to see so many church starts, and the good side of the emergent church is a joy to watch. But many established churches will not become a part of either of those movements. Or will they? But can the established churches be better versions of themselves? Is there a way to help them see the potential in themselves to change the planet? Like it or not, by 2020 we will know the answer.

So where are you in the "state of the church"? Think about the following statements: Which one fits you? Which one is the worst?

- You are in a box and are content to live there.

---

* See: www.visionnationals.org.

- You are free to live outside your box, but don't know how.
- You are in a box and think others should want in with you.

DISCUSSION GROUP

I'll say it again. I suggest you find two or more friends and discuss what you have read. The best way I believe to do that is for each of you to go back and highlight the five questions or statements that God used to impact you in this last chapter. Then get together, order takeout, and sit and talk about why those words struck you and how God may be using them in your life.

You will see this same paragraph at the end of each chapter, because I think it is important to talk to others about what God is doing.

Chapter 3

Or Symbolic Change?

ARE WE REALLY WILLING to admit that we need new visible symbols? Are we so stuck that we just think we need to keep doing what we are doing and using the same symbols and sooner or later they will work? The old saying goes, "A broken clock is right twice a day." But who wants to be right only two out of 1,440 minutes?

INDIVIDUALLY

Change for the sake of change is not change. It is "same". Just different "same". Do you want to be the same or truly changed? Do we want to change our symbols or do we just want symbolic change? Think before you answer. Because if you want change, you will need to drop some fairly ingrained ideas of what is right and what is wrong. You will need to learn some new thought processes. A friend of mine has a saying, "Never try to teach a pig to dance. It just won't work. And it annoys the pig." I am not saying you are a pig; I just don't want to annoy you. If you don't want to dance, say so now. Because real theological and ideological change must happen within you before it can happen in your church.

We do not necessarily need to trash our old symbols. Maybe we can dust them off and give them new meaning. The cross will never be irrelevant. But we can make it seem as though it is irrelevant. Our buildings do not have to be irrelevant use of funds during the week. Our processes and programs do not need to be non-producing. We could re-task them for use.

Can we start holding up a symbol which is not a visual but is highly visible? Is character as a daily visible enough to carry us forward?

HOW DID WE GET HERE?

So, to answer the question from the end of the last chapter—which is worse...

1. You are in a box and are content to live there.
2. You are free to live outside your box, but don't know how.
3. You are in a box and think others should want in with you.

If number one is your answer, you are lukewarm. If number two—you are willing, but stuck. But number three is the worst, because you are deceived. How many churches are number three? I pray we can find churches who will move from three to two and are willing to learn.

Many believers I talk to are just doing the last thing they were told to do. They are running a system. And, in many places, they're running it well. They do not know anything other than what they have seen and been taught to do. I am not assessing blame here. It is what it is. We have handed down a culture of church system through the last five or so generations. It worked at one time but no longer is giving the results the King is looking for. So we need to stop some things.

> There is nothing so useless as doing efficiently that which should not be done at all.
>
> —Peter F. Drucker

So why are we stuck where we are? I personally believe the genesis of the problem has its roots in three areas.

One—The fact that Sigmund Freud and friends took "soul care" out of the church and made helping people a profession. Not that I think we should do away with counselors. It is just that caring for people and loving people as we teach (disciple) them the ways of Christ is the church's main job.

Two—The church started growing large congregations in the industrialized cities and adopted systems to deal with problems caused by size.

Three—We adopted pragmatism as our main theology. The father of pragmatism, William James, would probably be disgusted with this.

You do not have to agree with these three to read further. This is just my opinion. I'm writing more about that in

2010—how we got where we are and our newest obses-
sion—including research and numeric values.

WE ARE BOXED UP

(NOTE: Think this through, as an individual and as a leader
in your church.)

You must first choose to realize that you are actually in a
box (not designed by you but inherited). You are not content,
and you have no clue as to how to get out of it. But, with all
that is in your being, you want to get out! If you don't, there
is no need to read further.

Once we admit that we are in a box and we are willing
to do whatever it takes to get out of that box, the rest is
a lot easier. Don't get me wrong. Boxes in and of themselves are not bad. Boxes can hold things together that are
good. Containers are important. As humans, once we have
accepted Christ, our lives are actually a container for God.
He lives in us. But we must not become a container that
rarely moves. We must be a container that moves about the
planet carrying what is good to those boxes that do not have
what is good. It is like Jesus going viral. We'll talk about that
in chapter twelve. If we can start thinking in that way, we
will have moved out of the "deceived" statement.

FOR THOSE WHO DO NOT KNOW CHRIST

For those who do not know Christ, the box represents the
fact that you are still "dead in your trespasses and sins." But

He is waiting for you to choose Him! For those of us who are now in a relationship with Christ, we are unboxed. Yet, for leaders in churches there is a tendency to build a new box. One we control. Therein lies the dilemma. We desire to help others get out of one box and into another. Is that really what we want to do? This puts people back in the same situation they were in before they became Christians. Yes they are going to heaven when they die, but they may die sooner due to being re-boxed.

Ephesians 2:1, 8, 9, 10 has a lot to say about this.

Ephesians 2:1 says, "you were dead in your trespasses and sins" (NAS). We were all born deceived and boxed.

Ephesians 2:8-9 says that "by grace you have been saved by faith" (NAS). Faith is not something we conjured up.

We are born in a spiritual box. God gives us the faith to get out of the box. So we cut out the lid and stand up. Christ hands us the box knife (faith) and helps us cut the lid out and stand up. It's almost like telling Lazarus to get up and come out of that grave. We become believers in Him. We breathe fresh spiritual air! Yet we are still standing in the box—only the lid was removed.

Once we see how great things are we try to move around the planet with new vision, but we take our box with us. We must allow Christ and the box knife to cut the sides down and allow us to run free again. Many times, once you cut the box sides and your box lays flat on the ground, you just stand there. You are free, but not moving.

What parts of the box (or your church's box) do you need to start disassembling?

As you start the change for your box or your church's box, you will get pushed back.

HAVE WE STOPPED GOING FOR THE BANANAS?

There is the story of the monkeys in a large cage who are squirted with a water hose while reaching for bananas up in a tree. As new monkeys are introduced into the cage, they each go for the bananas and are shot with water. After a while, the new monkeys are held back by the other monkeys who know there is no use trying. And they never try. You will just be hosed. And none of them knew the hose had been turned off. Have we become one of the monkeys? Are we stuck with some wrong knowledge?

"God's dreams of releasing you... releasing you to dream." Go for the bananas.

Bruce Wilkinson wrote a book called *DreamGiver*. In it he outlines how there are people who help us along our path toward where we are going and those who are hindrances. He calls them border busters or border bullies. When you get to certain borders, you need people who are going to help you cross into new lands, not those who will stop you from it.

I suggest you make sure it is God asking you to go for it. Sometimes the border bullies are there to make you rethink where you are going and why you are going there.

CAN WE REFOCUS OUR THEOLOGY?

> I make more mistakes than anyone else I know, and sooner or later, I patent most of them.
>
> —Thomas Edison

Edison got it. He knew that he needed to constantly rethink things. Are we willing to refocus and allow rethinking or redefining on a spiritual level?

How do we view God? Who do we think He is? Those are theological questions. How we answer them defines how we act on His behalf. As leaders, the answers then define how we go about "doing church." Can we rethink toward a relational theology—that God is a God of relationships? We tend to always say that He is a God of order. But we rarely say that He is a God of relationships. Can we allow and help people to become who God sees them to be? Think deeply about this next section. It will either help you in chapter four or you will need to come back and re-read it.

God has ideas for each person AND each church as a whole.

ποίημα "For we are His workmanship, created in Christ Jesus for good works, which God prepared beforehand so that we would walk in them" (Ephesians 2:10, NAS). Workmanship in Greek means "poem." He is writing our poems. One for each of us...it is our story. And our name, the name He has given us, is in His book, the Lamb's book of life. How do we know? Because that's what He tells us in Revelation 20:15.

God likes writing stories, not making lists.

Does God have some incredible ideas for your church, but because of your desires for His church, He cannot accomplish them? Has our theology or our ideology caused us to box people up instead of releasing them?

For the most part, it seems for us "to do church," we have extrapolated principles from the stories God has told us. We then have found pragmatic ways of measuring how to use those stories in our own lives. We watch closely the measurements to see if we have been a success. When we do this, we have lost the point of the stories.

God is writing a story of each of our lives. Our names are not "listed" in the Lamb's book of life; they are "written" in the Lamb's book of life. Satan has deceived us into thinking the book is a list—like Santa's. Satan's list—like Santa's list—is all about being naughty or nice. God's list is not a list at all. It is your story. It is the record of your poem much like the characters in the OT. The book of Ruth is not a list. It is an excerpt from her life. A part of her story which God felt we needed to know. So He had it written down and passed down.

So, not only is your name written down, there is a story to go with it. And that story is the relational deeds you do while on the planet.

CAN WE RETHINK OUR IDEOLOGY?

How we do what we believe we are to do.

The story He is writing is basically what we do as we respond to who He is in our lives. How do we understand what it is He has asked us to do? That is an ideological or methodological question. Ruth's story had all the details needed to convey it. That is because she followed Him and He had much to write about there. Her actions matched her belief in Him as her God.

For leaders: What story is God writing about your church? Does He have plans that you are thwarting with your agendas? What did He have in mind when the founders sensed that He wanted to start your church? Are you following and seeking to know what His plans are? Do you have different ideas than He does for your church? Is He actually at work while you are facing the other direction? He has called you by name. To what purpose has He called you? What name has He given you? Adam's purpose was to name the animals. God names and renames humans. What has He named you? Your church's purpose is in your story. To what purpose does He call you collectively? What did God promise your community when He started your church? You are free to go be that person and that church and do what you've been created to do. Let no one stop you. Not even you!

Yet...here you stand...back on that little piece of cardboard!

Jesus lived and lives outside the box...nothing confines Him. He is the definition of "life outside the box."

**What did God promise your community
when He started your church?**

Can you stop counting long enough to rethink and play the good version of the "What If" game? Can you describe WHAT it is God wants with no how, where, when, why, mores, most, or many? Once you can describe WHAT you believe, then you will be free to describe HOW you do it. That is your theology and your ideology.

DISCUSSION GROUP

Now I mean it. I suggest you find two or more friends and discuss what you have read. The best way I believe to do that is for each of you to go back and highlight the five questions or statements that God used to impact you in this last chapter. Then get together, order takeout, and sit and talk about why those words struck you and how God may be using them in your life.

You will see this same paragraph at the end of each chapter, because I think it is important to talk to others about what God is doing.

Chapter 4

reSymbol:
More Than Rethink

THIS BOOK IS NOT a set of directions. You did not buy a box with reSymbol in it which includes directions and a schematic. Batteries are not included. But, there are some drawings and pictures. Finding "directions" means the manufacturer designed something and intends that it be put together exactly as stated. Unfortunately, the person typing the instructions was not the person making the product. So there were parts or steps missing, or both, which added frustration.

My point in the set of reSymbol tools is to give you some practical spiritually diagnostic tools and show you basically how to use them.

INDIVIDUALLY

Much of the time I observe Christians behaving as if they have no mind. They cannot think for themselves. I want you to think for yourself and personally give up some habits you do without even thinking. We can rethink things all day long. I do. I explain to myself why I should start or stop something. Yet I seem to fall in the same habit the next day. Personal change is not as easy as just reading a verse and then doing it. If that were the case, then my Bible drill days would have been glorious. I know a lot of verses. I need to know my Lord more. I need for Him to change me. I need to give up thinking I can rethink it and reorganize it and reprioritize it. What things come to mind that you want to change, but just either can't or see no need to? Either way, I think Christ Himself wants to help. As you read this chapter, see if you can catch yourself doing the three things in your own life.

CURRENT SYMBOLS

Our current symbols of success—those numbers which show our victories—are waning. We have relied on the numeric symbols of buildings and budgets and Sunday School numbers to do the work of the ministry of the church, within the church. This is oddly similar to Israel, thinking that the ark would do the work of achieving victory against the Philistines in 1 Samuel 4. Yet Israel was severely defeated and the ark lost for 20 years. We have an ark, just as they did. Is it lost? Remember that Israel's treating of the ark as an "it" (1 Samuel 4:3) preceded not only the loss of the ark but also the birth of the one named Ichabod. You sure do not want that name above the door of your ministry or church.

At this point you must decide if you are willing to take a soul-searching journey to find your ark (symbols) which you have put in place instead of following Him. We have forgotten it is the "ark of the covenant." They too had forgotten the covenant part of the statement. We have designed systems and models that seem to work and they have become our ark. We have forgotten our real reason for existence. The church has become a WHAT and a WHERE and forgotten we are a WHO. We have been comparing our WHATS.

I had a boss years ago who told me, "Half of knowing what you want to do is knowing what you don't want to do." That applies somewhat here. Half of knowing what you should be doing is also knowing what you shouldn't. There are three things I see regularly in all shapes and sizes of churches. Three things that churches need to stop. Three things you personally may need to stop.

STOP DOING AT LEAST THREE THINGS:

Quit Comparing His Church Parts

Figure 1. Even when change is accepted as a possibility, we

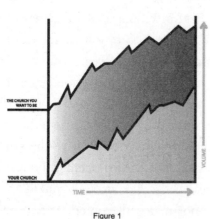

Figure 1

always compare up. We are always "keeping up with the Joneses." The proverbial Joneses always have more. Why do we never see the Joneses having less? Why do we always focus on the "church

Joneses" as having more? Because we are focusing on the wrong symbols. Comparison hasn't really worked well. And if it were working now, we would not be having these conversations. If comparison worked, you would simply need to close the gap between you and them by doing what they have done.

We never see Him call His church by the parts. He only names them by location. Like the church at Ephesus. We make the distinctions so clear with our titles and denominations that silo walls have been erected and standing tall for years. We have defined ourselves in ways He never intended. We call them distinctions. I believe He thinks they stink. His desire is that we be one. Read John 17:22 (NAS): "The glory which You have given Me I have given to them, that they may be one, just as We are one." His desire is that the walls which divide come down. That we be more universal and actually pull off Acts chapter 2.

Quit Frankensteining His People

Immediately you knew what I am talking about. Frankenstein was barely alive, didn't communicate very well, and all the villagers wanted to kill him. When we piecemeal our church structure in an attempt to make us look like the best parts of all the other churches we want to be like, we end up with the bride of Frankenstein not the bride of Christ. Though we can sew the parts together, they do not have the same DNA. So the internal structure doesn't match. Typically parts have a philosophical basis they are built on. If that philosophical basis does not match the other parts, it will not work. It will only make matters worse, and that part will end up getting rejected. This is why doctors spend so much time making sure a donated organ is a match in all ways before they do surgery. Organ rejection can be fatal, as can sticking the wrong parts together within a body of believers. It's like using a 1962 Cadillac™ headlight to replace your broken 2008 Chevrolet™ headlight. You end up with more of a Frankenstein situation than you intend.

We compare and piecemeal while attempting to emulate those who have more and seem to have it working with their ark. So long as this is a model, we will not reSymbol.

Frankenstein was barely alive, didn't communicate very well, and all the villagers wanted to kill him.

As Baptists, we say we believe "autonomy" and the "priesthood of the believer." Yet we try to look like other churches. And everyone in our church has to march to the same drum. Individualism is discouraged.

Quit Squeezing His Bride

It is not our job to hold tightly to His bride. We squeeze the life out of her much of the time. It is God's job to put the squeeze on us. We are the bride. He squeezes the life INTO us. Jeremiah 18:1–4 calls Him "the potter." A Hebrew listening to Jeremiah at that time would not have thought of the noun potter. He would have thought of the verb form of the word. He would have mentally visualized a "squeezer into shaper." Much like this. We visualize an airline pilot with his uniform on, saying goodbye to us after the flight. An Old Testament Hebrew would visualize the "flyer of the plane." They much more saw the name as what someone did or a major characteristic they exhibited. We should not attempt to hold on tightly to His bride.

I think we attempt too much of the time to squeeze the bride into the shape WE want her to be. We have a western mind-set and we visualize what we want, then we do all we can to squeeze people into that mold for our sake. But since this is the bride of Christ, it is a dangerous place to be. Control is a real issue.

THOSE THREE ARE THE A-TO-B AXIS

The three things to stop represent three ways we attempt to go from being church A to being church B. There are probably more than three things we need to stop, but these three cover much of what I have seen over the years. Our desire for control and the power that comes with that control can corrupt even the purest motives.

> A fondness for power is implanted, in most men, and it is natural to abuse it, when acquired.
> —Alexander Hamilton, "The Farmer Refuted,"
> February 23, 1775

If a controlled, perfected church management system with precise checks and balances is what God intended, then he would have sent an accountant and an engineer instead of Jesus. Now there is nothing wrong with accounting and engineering. They are valuable professions where gifted people work. I know a few of them. I could have used just about any profession here and shown how we have allowed it to overrule God's relational desires in our lives. Relationships should cross all professions. God just does not do things according to the books or according to our rules. He whittled Gideon's army down to the point they would HAVE to have God show up. He confused everyone by saving Paul the apostle. Jesus continually drove the Pharisees crazy by breaking all their rules. He is not interested in rules, but relationships. Not duty, but desire to be one with Him and His desires.

We should not attempt to hold on tightly to His bride.

By stopping at least "these three things" I believe we can put ourselves in a position to start with a new focus. An outward-sending focus that will help us all and then restructure some of our thinking.

START BECOMING X-TO-Y—FOCUS OUT

This is probably NOT about outreach as you define it in your mind. So, drop that definition. In changing our strategy from the A to B axis to an X to multiple Y axis, we become seed planters, not gatherers. Much like what Jesus taught was about decentralizing. It was about going, not gathering. Yes I know "we are not to forsake the gathering together" (Hebrews 10:25).

I am not saying that we do away with the gathering. We just gather too much and scatter too little. And if we do scatter, we do not know our purpose while we are scattered. We think it is about us. I am asking, as individuals and groups, do we go? Do we start new things where new things need to be started? Are we seed scatterers or "seed Nazis"— like the "Soup Nazi" from *Seinfeld*? Can success be redefined by going, not staying? By leaving, not gathering? Can our measuring tools be redefined to also include starting new works? Or starting new ministries? Or sending people out? Can we actually rely less on our measuring tools? I wonder what Christ would think of our "gathering" techniques when He clearly instructed us using "sending" techniques. Large gatherings did not seem to excite him as much as they do us. What seemed to excite Him was people following Him and "living a sent life."

In **Figure 2**, church A-to-B is a church which has found 10 things another church is doing. They want to be like that

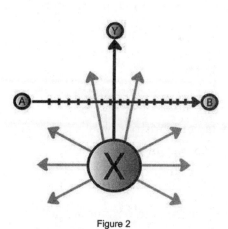

Figure 2

church, so they just attempt to start doing those 10 things. An X-to-Y church sees itself as mobile and effective during the week. We grow large by growing out. By being distributed all over the planet during the week. All over. All week. It is allowed to express itself in ways it can to reach those they come in contact with during the week. Their gatherings are intentional relational discipling—including during the sermons in worship times. (NOTE: I am again reminded how we are not concerned with discipling. Even that word comes up with a red line under it, noting that it is not a recognized word in the dictionary. And so it is within many churches.)

If a controlled, perfected church management system with precise checks and balances is what God intended, then he would have sent an accountant and an engineer instead of Jesus.

All the arrows could have a "Y" or whatever. They are destinations, relationships, new plants, new church expressions, or new addresses where the church meets—the places you GO where you see the people you impact.

To begin the reSymboling process, we have to revisit and answer some of those questions:

- What are your symbols of success—the church—the life of Christ?
- Of all your symbols, which ones take the most of your time, your energy, your effort, and your money?
- Which ones are actually important to you?
- How do you know you are doing what God is asking?
- What are the unwritten rules which you adhere to but have no affect on the success of your church?
- A-to-B does not work...then the Dr. Phil question fits here. "So how is that working for you?" If A-to-B is not it, then what?

You must decide that you and your church will follow the other axis, which is actually not an axis but a set of arrows pointing out.

Then the question becomes, do you talk about it or do it? Do you talk about arrows or ARE you arrows? Nothing is stopping you but YOU. We are told to train up a child in the way he should go (according to their bent) and also told that when he is old he will not depart from it. That verse refers to shooting an arrow. Each arrow is bent and will fly in a certain way and in a certain direction. We could use that same verse and, in a way, apply it to a church. Train us, a church in the way it should go! Point it in the right direction and let it fly!

Can you take the arrows from the X-to-Y church and make them point in the same direction?*

The point to the last set of questions is this: It is not that you actually want everyone going in the same direction—just coming from the same basis or sources and headed for the same purpose. When arrows start moving in other directions, you know that they are doing the same things other ministries are, just in different ways. In this way we can fish different parts of the planet without all having to be in the same boat.

I wonder what Christ would think of our "gathering" techniques when He clearly instructed us using "sending" techniques.

Too much of the time we either follow the leader or we are the leader who only wants others to hold on to the rope behind the boat. In either case, the leader's power and desires pull the followers around the lake as they attempt to fish that

---

* See: www.ReleasingChurches.org.

lake. There are also leaders who desire to set people free in their own boats and give them what they need to successfully fish the lake. There is value in both models. But, if you want to cover the whole lake as soon as possible and as efficiently as possible, releasing people into their own boats and sending them off to different parts of the lake to fish would be the better option.

DISCUSSION GROUP

By this meeting, change your takeout menu. Pizza is getting old. I still suggest you find two or more friends and discuss what you have read. I still think the best way to do that is for each of you to go back and highlight the five questions or statements that God used to impact you in this last chapter. Then get together, order something besides pizza, and sit and talk about why those words struck you and how God may be using them in your life.

You will see this same paragraph at the end of each chapter, because I think it is important to talk to others about what God is doing.

Chapter 5

Invisible Realities

L ET ME START OUT by saying that this has been on my mind for over 15 years. God is more interested in the invisible part of my life than He is in the visual part of my life. My question, one individual to another is this: Are you concerned in the same ways He is?

INDIVIDUALLY

Much of my life I tried to keep the externals correct, while the internals crumbled. And growth of anything good was going on inside. I had my believer's game face on. Do you? What do you hold up for others to view instead of letting them see the real you as you change to look more like Christ? Just a question. Keeping up appearances is just that. Keeping up appearances. This has been going on for some time.

Relational realties are invisible because that's the way God wants it. Jesus had a discussion with a woman at a well. When she perceived that He was a prophet, she launched into a discussion about where people should worship. This is kind of like when I am on a plane and through conversation the person next to me and I end up in a spiritual discussion. It is fine until they find out I believe in Christ or am a pastor. They immediately start talking about how they used to go to a (name the denomination) church when they were a kid. Or how their mom sings at weddings. Or they have an uncle who used to light candles. Anything to show that they are a religious person.

It is interesting how Jesus handles her statement. He tells her that soon worship will not have to take place in any particular location. You will worship in "spirit and truth" (John 4:24). Two things that are invisible. She wanted to discuss something concrete and visual; He wanted to talk about the eternal relational realities.

When talking with people, I usually agree with their frustrations about church. That seems odd to them. They then ask if I go to church. I tell them I do...but actually I AM the church. I then get that so-you're-part-of-a-cult look. Then I explain it. It's funny.

People who are not church attendees get the whole "spirit and truth" thing better than many church folks.

THE NEW SYMBOL—
THE CHARACTER OF CHRIST

If you can stop thinking about those three things in the last chapter long enough to consider the invisible realities of life, then you can use this to move to the next step—how to make the invisible, visible. As you go, there are certain relational realities that you must stay constantly mindful of. The character of Christ must show through us, all day, every day, in every relationship. At least that is His desire. And everything we do as believers in groups or gatherings must focus on that. Remember, He asked us to disciple as we go, everywhere we go. So we stop doing at least three things and start thinking "face out" and get beyond our box. And then go that way. In doing so, what symbols do we take? Character. After all, isn't God conforming us to His image (Romans 8:29)? So how does that work? Change. One flow to another.

RELATIONAL CHARACTER

THE GREAT CHARACTER FLOW
Isaiah 55:10-11

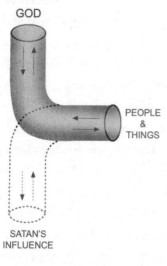

Figure 3

Figure 3. You are represented by the grey tube. In this illustration, you are a believer of Christ and you have an old relationship with Satan (dotted line tube) – since you were born with him as your father (John 8:44; Ephesians 2:1). The "PEOPLE" in your life are either believers or non-believers. They have either chosen to follow Christ or they have chosen not to follow Christ. And there are

"THINGS" which represent all the stuff God has given you to "steward." God is where you get all that you have to give away. What we communicate to others and how we use our "stuff" will communicate to them who God is. In Isaiah 55:10, the "bread for the eater and seed for the sower" represent something that nourishes us and something we can give away which will bring the same nourishment. What has God given you that He intends that you give away? Verse 11 explains that His word (His characteristics, qualities, and attributes) are to be given in the same way. In this way His character flows through you into the lives of others. And vice versa.

Make no mistake. Satan will try to influence you all he can. But as a believer you only have a distant relationship with him. He is no longer your father. God is your father. Nevertheless, Satan will try to divert your attention from God by using whatever means he can come up with. He will come at you personally at times. Other times he will use people and things. Sometimes the very things you are trying to use as a good steward for the sake of others. And he will attempt to use the very people you are attempting to influence.

Where and when does all this take place? All day. Every day. This spiritual reality is never at rest. It is always in existence. We either are involved in it positively or negatively. God's desire is that we live life thinking about Him and how we affect other people. This spiritual reality takes place on the physical plane of life and earth. So all that we have can be used by us for Him to impact all the others He puts in our lives. Do we steward it well or do we spend most of it on ourselves? Sure, we are supposed to tithe a tenth and let the organized church decide where that goes. But shouldn't you be involved in deciding where that goes? And should we all not use the remaining 90% for those around us? Yes. Stating the obvious, that is a tough pill to swallow.

RELATIONAL INTENTIONALITY

THE GREAT COMMISSION
Matthew 28:19-20

What do you think Jesus meant when He said GO?

Figure 4. (See: www.ReleasingChurches.org.) As you see in the web graphic, Figure 3 morphs into Figure 4. You ARE

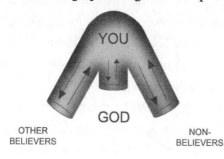

Figure 4

Figure 4 and God's intention is that you intentionally allow His character to flow through you into the lives of others no matter where you are, using (stewarding) what you have to make that happen. But are you doing that? Are you intentionally asking yourself who is at the end of your focus and what are you doing to genuinely care for them? How are you to do that? Why are we all doing church the way we are doing it? That verse has been called The Great Commission for years. We are commissioned. Doesn't commissioning mean you are going somewhere? Don't people who are commissioned, leave? Not stay? Think about this. Go is actually used as a participle in Matthew 28:19, which actually means "go" and "as you go." "As you are commissioned...." But it has an imperative feel to it. So He means "GO" and "as you go" at the same time. It has intentionality. What part of your life are you not "as you are going"? Also, the word "make" is an added word in the English language to turn the noun mathetes into a verbal clause. In the original Greek mathetes was a verb. We have taken the word make and used it as a manufacturing term. So then we need a manufacturing plant (the church building) and a manufacturing system (our processes and programs).

(NOTE: I am not saying we stop all our processes. I am saying we use the worship/discipleship/stewardship systems we can to deliver the message of character flow into the other 160+ hours a week when we are NOT at the buildings. What if you had no buildings? You would still need to gather and then go. Gather then go. Gather then go. Gather then go.)

Add to this Acts 1:8, "But you will receive power when the Holy Spirit has come upon you; and you shall be my witnesses both in Jerusalem, and in all Judea and Samaria, and even to the remotest part of the earth." This verse takes the "as you go" to everywhere.

Your worship is your constant recognition that you have a relationship with Him and that He is who supplies all your needs. Your discipleship is your relationship with the people now (believers and non-believers) in your life. Some of the people you are influencing you do not even know yet, and may never know. Your stewardship is using what things He has given you for those two sets of relationships. If you have children, your job is to be responsible and show them how to be Christ themselves. They are supposed to leave your house someday and go help be a positive Christ influence on the planet too. The world should see that God is in you. The intent should be worshipping/discipling/stewarding—168 hours a week.

RELATIONAL COMMUNITY
THE GREAT COMMANDMENT
Matthew 22:34-40

Figure 5. The flow of the character of God runs through us and to us. In community! We are commanded to love people.

Figure 5

So anytime we do not love people, we are disobeying the greatest commandment of all. This loving community is what Acts 2 looked like. We do not do this on our own. We can't. We are not designed to. We must do this together. God has designed us for relational community. And what the church today can look like. The characteristic listed in the Matthew passage is love. We must let our people free and "send them" to be in context every day where they come in contact with a world that needs love. Not as a predetermined duty or with the end in mind to "get them to church." As people are at work standing there near the water cooler or in their office cubicle, they ARE the church. We must intentionally be with the ones we love and learn to love the ones we are with.

For years I led people to believe that we all served a church on Sunday. I forgot to show them how to serve a King all week.

Living in community (as a verb not a place) is just foreign to us. We have become so self-dependent that we really have not thought too much about needing other people in our lives, much less living with them deeply in our lives in loving relationships which expose where we do not look like Christ.

I have found myself more and more wanting to help people to live this verse and all of Acts 2. Yet I keep thinking, "How do I measure their success?" Why do I feel that I must do that? It is just what I have been taught. You know SAM—goals which are Specific, Attainable, and Measurable.

The problem with love is that we can't measure it. Does it count then?

We have His character, are commissioned to go, and commanded to love. Do we? What would an outsider say to that?

CONSTANT CONNECTION

So, we have three items to think about. God, people, and things. Thinking of those three items raises three simple questions: How do we worship God? How do we disciple people? How do we steward the things He has given us to do both? Shouldn't all churches work from the same three?

Worship, Discipleship, and Stewardship.

We love God and we love others, using all that we have to do both.

Worship

It is not an event or destination, but a reminder of who He is in our lives. A way of living so that Jesus is your focus every day. You see who He is and His character more each day through the world, the Word, and other believers. But don't stop gathering to collectively worship. Corporate worship should be a celebration of what God has done in the past and expectation of what He will do in the future.

Discipleship

Bible studies don't make disciples. Disciples make disciples. An intentional daily walk with others in your path so that His character flows is your foremost thought. This is the base intent of the Great Commission. It is transformation (Romans 12). It is allowing God to conform you to the image of His Son. It is Spiritual Formation. By this, you infect the others—believers and non-believers—by exhibiting the character you see in Him. Make discipleship a way of life. But don't stop gathering in groups. Any group time should always have as part of it a celebration of what God has done and what He will do in the future. Discipleship includes evangelism. As a follower of Christ, you are teaching people about who He is by how you act and what you say. So, actually, you are doing unintentional evangelism each day without knowing it. A good question to regularly ask yourself is, "Who do you know who doesn't know WHO you know?" Those people are watching you. You are teaching them about Christ. What are you teaching them? Do you ever intentionally talk to them about Him and your life with Him?

Stewardship

Not just a tithe. You and the church collectively using what it has for the sake and well being of others. Use it all to show them His character. We emphasize our buildings too much for our use. We need to use them for the community. But don't stop tithing. Start using the other 90% of what you have as individuals for the sake of others.

> Not everything that can be counted counts, and not everything that counts can be counted.
> —Albert Einstein

We need to help people learn again there is a flow of who He is into the lives of others. Those seeds of his character are to be planted.

This is not a new paradigm; not a paradigm shift. It is a Doctrine of Relationships. It has a reciprocal part to it that Figures 3 and 4 imply. It assumes you are asking questions of connection, not duty. It is a clothesline on which to hang our theology and our practice. No one exists who is not around God. Are we then being the others in their lives? If we can't explain what we are doing using the relational triangle, should we be doing it? If we cannot demonstrate how what we are doing is "loving people," should we be doing it?

Those three diagrams are simply the invisible way the flow of character is to work. The tubes represent connections that exist. And where they meet is where the stewardship of material things takes place, as well as the "character exchange." We are either getting better at it or not doing so well.

There are many other diagrams which explain blockage of flow. How Satan works in the midst of it all tying to shut down the fellowship connections. There is how individual relationships either help or hinder spiritual growth, the six planes of life. Why there is only one set of dotted lines, etc. But that's another book. Maybe I'll call it "Tubular Theology."

DISCUSSION GROUP

At this meeting I suggest you grill out. And what you need to grill is bratwurst in keeping with the tubular theme. I still suggest you find two or more friends and discuss what you have read. I still think the best way to do that is for each of you to go back and highlight the five questions or statements that God used to impact you in this last chapter. Then get together, grill out, and sit and talk about why those words struck you and how God may be using them in your life.

You will see this same paragraph at the end of each chapter, because I think it is important to talk to others about what God is doing.

Chapter 6

The Invisible Visible

S o, THIS IS HOW I think Jesus thinks it should work. It is all about relationships. That is our purpose. But how do we organize it?

INDIVIDUALLY

This is a tough one. How do you ask someone individually to work through this without them being in a church setting, where it is being worked through collectively? That is a dilemma. Many times in the OT God asked prophets and regular Joes to walk according to His ways. They were out of step with society and with the other Israelites. But they followed God. I guess what I am asking here is that you take up the banner and seek to find ways that you can sincerely ask the six questions of yourself and then lead the charge as you change.

We sometimes have so much going on at such a rate of speed that when someone suggests something different, we say it can't be done. We have so encumbered Him and His word we can't see our way out of the entanglement of the woods to live free. In *My Utmost for His Highest*, Oswald Chambers says on January 26th, "A simple statement of Jesus is always a puzzle to us because we will not be simple... By receiving His Spirit, recognizing and relying on Him, and obeying Him as He brings us the truth of His Word, life will become amazingly simple."*

How have we missed it? I believe it is our layers of pragmatism, our egos and our sinful comparative natures which lead us to an unhealthy desire to be recognized. Yes that hurts. Pride goes before the fall. Will you fall or change? Can you refocus your theology and rethink your ideology? Can you simplify it enough to get back to original WHO and His WHAT?

SIX THINGS TO START ASKING

(NOTE: I am not suggesting doing away with Sunday School or worship, but to rethink how we do all of this.)

When working through these six things, you must be willing to take them personal. And as a servant leader, you must be willing to get your best leaders from all age groups to have some intelligent discussions with no emotional outbreaks. They must take seriously the fact that they want to go back to the Bible and ask some serious questions about the methods and any unwritten rules that "run" their church.

---

* http://www.rbc.org/devotionals/my-utmost-for-his-highest/01/26/devotion.aspx.

Think of the following in this way. The earth has a core and layers upon that core. The center core of this analogy is the WHO. Each of the other words are layers on top of the center core.

As you think through this next section, picture this illustration in your mind—the layers of the Earth. The core is the WHO, then the WHAT all the way out to the WHERE. Six layers. Six things to rethink... reSymbol.

Who, What, Why, How, When, Where

- Who—who is at the center of your church?
- What—what do you do with the who?
- Why—why do you do that?
- How—how do you do that?
- When—when do you do that?
- Where—where do you do that?

(If your staff can agree and lead/teach the first three, you can then allow the bride—including you—to be free to follow and create the last three.)

As we break these down, we must start with the WHO. The following is the short version of the answers I believe God would give if He were answering.

WHO?—Jesus is the center with the Father and the Holy Spirit. Everything is built upon them.

You and the WHO—Jesus. If Jesus is not the center of your church or your life, you need not go any further. None of these other layers will make any sense. It will be like building your house on sand. And we all know how well that works (Matthew 7:24-26). We seem to SAY we've built our churches on Jesus and what He says. But in reality, we have built our churches on the sands of pragmatism. And He is not at the center. We are. With our desire and controls. The question for us then becomes, are we going to change who is at the center and then assist people in the growing flow of the character of Jesus as they go about their lives? Is Jesus the center of their lives? If not, He is not the collective center of our church either. We have become so event- and project-oriented that it is hard to figure out how to help them focus on Jesus and the 165 hours they are not at our building or attending something we planned.

The layers on top of the WHO are layers that must allow Him to shine through. Sometimes they are so thick people can only see the layers, not Jesus.

WHAT?—If Jesus is really the WHO of your church, then He should have some say, the final say, on what the WHAT is. It really is simple. Based on the two verses many of us seem to land on, the Great Commission and the Great Commandment are worship, discipleship, stewardship. But we have just added so much to these three that we don't even recognize them anymore. Without even knowing it, we seem to have become like the Pharisees. They had preconceived ideas on what should be done—how and where and when. Jesus undid all of that. They did not like it. But our Father has seen fit to write it down so we could look at it closely and daily. If this confuses you, go back and read the Great Commission and the Great Commandment. Ask God to show you the many parameters you and others have added to them. I hope you will be as shocked as I am when I ask God to show me. It is quite spiritually embarrassing sometimes when He shows me something I'm doing and I am insisting that it is THE way to do it. He opens my eyes to how much I have added to His truth. At that point, my only recourse is to say, "Father, forgive me, I am sorry. Help me to understand You and Your ways better and to not add to what You have said."

WHY?—"So that...", or "In order that..."

The answers I regularly get are answers which start with "because." "Because Jesus told me to." Or, "Because the leadership said we should." All the answers start with, "Because." There seems to be very little argument here. Until I start asking people to see if they can answer it starting the sentence with, "So that...," or "In order that...." If you can answer it in this way, it starts the thought processes moving toward the HOW.

Is Jesus the center of their lives? If not, He is not the collective center of our church either.

Starting a sentence with the word "because" sounds too much like my mother. When I had a question I did not want her to start her answer with, "Because...." That meant

I really wasn't going to get an explanation of why. I was going to get a static reason. Which I did not understand, or I would not have been asking the question in the first place. I do know why my mother did that. I asked too many questions and she was exhausted. But that ability to "question" life is paying off now. So, I am asking you now to think beyond the same theological answers and start moving the answers into a sentence with action steps that have real verbs in them. So, the next question actually starts taking us into the HOW.

Can we help people to gather and purpose it in such a way so that worship, discipleship, and stewardship are a natural part of their lives—individually and through purposeful gathering?

HOW?—through structures of intentional gathering and individually "as you go" lovingly, living sent. Your intentional gatherings are for worship and discipling, or events for similar purposes.

Here is where things start getting sticky. We will spend a chapter on this later because people can generally agree on the WHO-WHAT-WHY. But when we get to the HOW, everybody has an opinion. And they do not agree sometimes.

How did Jesus disciple or how do you disciple? That is the big question right here. Here we define HOW we do what Jesus has asked us to do. But it is also the HOW we communicate it. HOW we decide where the authority/ responsibility/accountability is. HOW we lead it. HOW we train leaders. HOW we release people.

This is why I started ReleasingChurches.org. It seemed to me that the HOW was so centralized and confining that it led to problems with the WHERE and the WHEN. So, my hopes are to unbox all believers who are presently boxed up. I want to free them to roam the planet daily and live in the midst of culture and those who don't know Christ in such a way they disciple daily!!

(NOTE: If you do not communicate what you now intend, you will get something different than what you intend. BUT if you do not DO what you say, it really doesn't matter what you communicate.)

Within the HOW you will find all that takes the WHO-WHAT-WHY and puts it in the WHERE-WHEN. Try not to put any WHERE-WHEN statements here unless God has given you a vision or direction. There are no verses quoted in the next section. You know what portions of scripture your group/denomination/gathering thinks are important to base things on. I have already given you the basic texts I believe God is asking us to accomplish. I am not going to argue those denominational points. I will argue that He has made it simple, and we have complicated it. So it is OUR job to disassemble things so that we can reSymbol. You must wrestle with that yourselves. First you decide:

1. Servanthood/Staffing

There is a WHO within the HOW. Where do you fit? How does your church decide leadership? Is it spiritual or spirit-led ritual, or has the spirit departed and all you have left is just ritual? Does this structure, coupled with voting rights, strangle any potential change? You must ask these tough questions if you hope to ever get past the HOW. You can use *StrengthsFinder 2.0* (a book which also has online testing) to see if who sits where are even functioning in their strengths as God has made them.* But if they are not spiritual people, it doesn't really matter. "Alignment and Cohesion Questionnaire" should be administered here (www.ReleasingChurches.org). I wrote these based on simple biblical principles. They are designed to see where everyone is, and if they are facing in the same direction. Who does what job; pecking order; who holds who accountable to what part of the WHAT and HOW; how all of the differing "how's" fit together; the reason for the WHEREs and WHENs and how they fit together. The WHO-WHAT-WHY can generally be agreed upon. But HOW each person interprets the verses into practice and who gets to be in charge of that will show up right here. It can get ugly if people do not generally trust each other and plan to walk this path together as brothers and sisters in love with Jesus and each other. Does the church as a whole feel that these are the right people to be serving them? If it all becomes about voting and control, you need to back up to the "squeezing the bride" part of chapter four. If you can't get past that, it will be hard to move beyond where you are. There may be a split or just people leaving regularly out of disgust. You may even have a heated church split and then name the new church "Friendship Church."

---

* Tom Rath, *StrengthsFinder 2.0: A New and Updated Edition of the Online Test from Gallup's Now, Discover Your Strengths* (New York: Gallup Press, 2007).

2. Worship

Is it relational? Is Christ visible in your worship? Is your God a person or an item of worship? What do participants hear? Do they think worship only happens at pre-appointed times? When you gather for worship, do you celebrate "what Jesus has done" since the last time you met? Ephesians 5:19-20 says, "Speak to one another with psalms, hymns and spiritual songs. Sing and make music in your heart to the Lord, always giving thanks to God the Father for everything, in the name of our Lord Jesus Christ." These two verses are referring to life in general, not a worship service. Are we living life that way? Are we integrating it into our corporate worship experience? Are your worship announcements more than a report of numbers? Are stories of changed lives a part of your worship? You must celebrate what you expect. What does the pastor announce and emphasize? That is what everyone will think is important. Does your worship focus on God or people? Do you spend time in genuine prayer, or is it rote? Is your song choice based on preference? Probably, most of it is. But does that preference sincerely say to Him how we feel about Him? Is your worship relational or functional? Is there more habit than reality? Is it about God/Jesus/Holy Spirit as persons and not as facts or truths? Do we worship truth as a person or a rational thought?

I will argue that He has made it simple, and we have complicated it.

Worship is more than music before the preaching. Worship is a lifestyle of seeing God in everything. He is around us. He is at work. But for the sake of your gathering time, let's stick to just that discussion. Is it about noise? Predictable? Do you follow the same flow you have for the last 300 weeks? Are people expecting to meet God there? Or are they there for the show? Have you attempted to prepare a gathering time which points toward Him or are you just trying to fill that hour? What are you telling them that worship is? You ARE telling them something by the way it is lead. Tell them it is about Him.

I did a little impromptu study when I was at First Baptist Church Moore outside Oklahoma City. We were about to start another worship service and we were trying to decide the style of music. That is usually like picking a fight in established churches. I got an idea to ask our senior adults what their favorite songs were. My list had about ten on it. Here were the top three. "How Great Thou Art," "Just As I Am," "Have Thine Own Way." Great songs. The thing I noticed about their choices was that they loved to sing songs TO God more than songs ABOUT God. So do we simply sing songs about Him and practice them until we have them perfect, or do we sing to Him regardless of how well we do? Is music a practice or sung to a person?

Our nature as followers is to want to worship Him. So it is less about song choices and more about direction choices. I am not saying that you only sing songs TO Him and never sing confessional songs ABOUT Him. The old saying "that we focus our heart's affection and our mind's attention on

Him" is right. If we have gathered for any other reason, it is just a gathering, not a worship gathering.

3. Discipleship/Literature for Individual and Groups

The Bible and the Holy Spirit must be first on the list. If that is not the base, there is no need go any further. Who chooses? Does it support the WHAT in a relational way? Does it give people something to do as they go and then encourage them to celebrate it with the group the next time they meet? Does it help them to be more relationally connected to Him as they go? Literature chosen must be more than intellectually informative. Worship must be instructive—explanatory at times. But above all, the literature must be expectantly relational. Does it ask questions that have more to do with clichés, thoughts, and facts than it does with emotions and feeling? Which of those is love? It sure shouldn't be a cliché, just a fact or an intellectual thought. God meant more than that when He said that He "so loved the world that he gave his one and only Son."

Do we worship truth as a person or a rational thought?

When I was over the education ministry at First Baptist, Orlando, I used to tell my teachers that I did MBWA (Management By Walking Around). At that time, all of our LIFE Groups met on campus on Sunday. I would stand outside one of the doors to the classroom and listen to the discussion going on. This unnerved some of them, but they got used to the fact that I was not critiquing them. I just wanted to help them to be relational in their teaching. I told them I just wanted to make sure they knew, "Real teachers teach people, not lessons."

If it is not relational, it is informational. God never gives us information for the sake of the information. He always informs us because of His love and care. He may even withhold info sometimes. That's another story. Our job within the use of literature, even the Bible, is to strengthen the relationship between God and people and between each other. If it does not do that, it is information.

Real teachers teach people, not lessons.

---

4. Stewardship/Property/Buildings

How do we use our buildings and our funds if we have them? When people are on your property, what is communicated to them? Is it well kept? Formal? Restrictive? Messy? Unkempt? Disorderly? Does it look like you care? Does it communicate what you are trying to communicate? Unfortunately, we have asked our buildings and properties to do the work of relationship in the past. We've "got to get 'em here so they can get saved." Then we hope it will happen. We don't do the "as you go" work before they show up. The early Christians pulled all of this off with no buildings. But since you do have a building, do you steward it well? I don't mean, is it a museum which is well maintained? I mean, does is get used for the sake of the Kingdom as much as possible? Or do you use it only a few hours a week? Is the church checkbook more about the church members and their comfort or about programs or about going? Look at the church checkbook. What percentage is spent on building, maintenance, utilities, programs, and systems? How much is actually spent on loving others beyond your walls? Can your percentages of that go up as your people learn to go out? Remember, Jesus was more about sending than gathering.

5. Communication

This includes your website, your bulletin, your announcements, your posters in the building, your signage, your media purchases—everything that is used to communicate anything! In essence, everything you say, and everywhere you say it; it must say the same thing in the same way. Ask yourself this question: What do I think an outsider would say is important to us? Even in the way you keep your meeting space says a lot to people. Your choices of colors say things. But all that is more in the building/stewardship area. Here I am mostly talking about the verbal and intentional visual communications. Ask someone who does not know your church at all to come and look at everything and tell you what they think you think is important. Does that importance match what you WANT to be important now? You may say in meetings and have in your minutes that something is important. Then you only mention it from the pulpit every month. You may have even put a sign up some-where and have it on your website.

Also, EVERYTHING cannot be important. If everything is important, nothing is important. Making sure you have narrowed down the WHAT helps you focus on HOW you communicate it. I am not saying that you only communicate one thing, just don't attempt to communicate one hundred things. If you do choose to pick one thing, make it Jesus.

6. The People

This is your main objective. Focus on the ones who are a part of the body of Christ, reaching out "as they go" and touching the ones who aren't. They are the parts of the layers, which are invisible so that Christ shines through them and the programs they might be a part of. The above 1–5 must be such that the people know exactly what "church" is all about.

What do you use the 1–5 for? I know all the answers. I have been in this long enough to have seen it all. What we tend to do is use the 1–5 to garner more gatherers. We sometimes say it is for sending, but the arrows seem to keep pointing back at us. Now, before you think I am railing at you, remember I am part of the problem. I have just been doing what I was told to do. I grew up in the system and it is a part of me. That is why I know it so well. Now I am trying to figure out how to help people in the system to redo the system so that it is pointed out. The problem is that the system is so interdependent and has such a low margin of excess funds to work with, it has problems looking out. We utilize people to maintain the system. I don't know who said it first, but I love this statement: "We have quit being fishers of men and become keepers of the aquarium." I think many people these days want out of the aquarium and want to go fishing themselves. Let's help them go.

All the unwritten rules become plain to see when you start rethinking your HOW. And some people will want to put some of those unwritten rules in writing, whether or not they fit the agreed upon who-what-why.

If there is only God and others, and God is always with us, then our only real question concerns how we affect others. If we truly intend on having a positive influence, then we must concern ourselves with how we use what we have and how we treat the others in our path. Knowing that what we do is for the King opens up His entire kingdom for us to serve.

WHERE?

That is your decision. Hopefully by now it is obvious that "as you go" is THE MAJOR where and when of people's lives. Is He visible through your people? The times and places the people of your church can "be" the church out where they are "is" most of their time. But you can't forget your gathering together places. Is He visible at your place of corporate worship? There is more WHERE out there than the spot you call church, but your place is important. Where you gather for worship says a lot about whom you are worshipping and who is worshipping with you.

Is the church checkbook more about the church members and their comfort or about programs or about going?

We get stuck here too sometimes. The word for church in the New Testament is ekklesia: "the called out ones." We are called out of our ways but are still living in society so that our new ways are obvious and point to Him. Nowhere is the word church used in the New Testament to mean a time or a place. Never. So how do we redefine "our church" so that it fits the biblical word Jesus used? It doesn't mean that we quit meeting or get rid of our building. We do need to be better stewards of what we have. I think we could use our building for more than just gathering disciples. How can you utilize what you have for the sake of the community in which you live?

WHEN?

Too much of the time, our choices for WHERE and WHEN are designed for containment and measurement. Our buildings, our calendars, and our overly planned worship times and Sunday school leave no room for God to do anything. What could He do if we released all that to Him? Its His anyway. As I've said, we are His 168 hours of the week. How many of them do we actually spend for Him and not for us?

Six words can ask a lot of questions and stir up a lot of spiritual angst. But if you want to go from where you are to where He wants you to be, then you must ask them. Or you will stay in the box.

DISCUSSION GROUP

At this meeting, for dessert, I suggest you have jawbreakers. These things are hard to get to the middle of. They have layers, which keep you from getting to the middle. I still suggest you find two or more friends and discuss what you have read. And yes, I still think the best way to do that is for each of you to go back and highlight the five questions or statements that God used to impact you in this last chapter. Then get together, order Chinese takeout, and sit and talk about why those words struck you and how God may be using them in your life.

You will see this same paragraph at the end of each chapter, because I think it is important to talk to others about what God is doing.

Chapter 7
Spiritual Mimes

W E'VE BECOME PARALYZED. WE go through the motions again and again with no visible effect. Do you still feel the sides of that box from chapter three? As leaders, do we box up our people for our purposes?

INDIVIDUALLY

How much of the time are you simply going through the motions? I ask myself that as well as you. Mimes are strange things to me. The good ones really are convincing. They make me think there is a rope, box, wall, whatever. How good are you at playing the part that something is really happening? How good are you at "selling it" so that you are fairly convinced that how you do what you do as a believer is actually what He wants and is good enough? Is there any kingdom impact because you are His? Do you ever say to yourself "Well that ought to be enough for right now?" You may not use those words, but your actions explain that you are basically just getting by with being the least Christian you can. I am saying these things to myself also. I spent much of my life running the system of church. The whole while I was doing very little to nurture the life of Christ within me or within others. Are you just "oiling the machine"? That question hurts me. I sensed God saying to me a couple of years ago, "Doug, you have served the church well, thank you... now I want you to serve the King." That doesn't mean I don't care about the church now; just more deeply and differently.

> Do not quench your inspiration and your imagination; do not become the slaves of your model.
> —Vincent Van Gogh

He was right. We are slaves to the model of the way we have done things.

When our HOW has so incased our WHAT, it becomes impossible to see the WHO. Therefore accomplishing the WHAT without the WHO is irrelevant.

You can think that same sentence through using the words WHERE and WHEN and even WHY in the place of HOW!

No wonder we can't reach people and help them become disciples of Jesus. With all the layers, they can't even see him.

Our obsessing with counting adds yet another layer.

We put 90% of our expectations on 1.79% (3/168ths) of the week.

What if we figured out new ways to attack the other 165 hours of the week that did not compromise the three hours on Sunday?

What if Sunday became a time of celebration for the past 165 hours and anticipation for the next 165?

What if we were sent by Christ to make a difference and the difference we made out there counted as much as our attendance "at church"? Or more?

As leaders, answer these questions:

- If your church buildings burnt to the ground and you were not allowed to rebuild, could you do church?
- Can you define success without using numbers, counting, or without using the words "more" or "most"?
- What is the purpose of the pastoral staff?
- Could congregants have bigger kingdom dreams than the staff? Who gets to define which dream gets built?
- What are the limiting factors we may have unconsciously put on ourselves?
- Are you asking those gathered to do God's work the way YOU want it done?
- When gathering people, how do you define when "enough gathering is enough"?

We put 90% of our expectations on 1.79% (3/168ths) of the week.

As a leader, have these questions crossed your mind:

- How can I release all those folks out there into the kingdom for His sake?
- Should I measure what and how they are doing?
- What do they want to do that has not come to their minds because they know that the answer will be NO?
- Do they think I have all the ideas?
- What "box" or "model" are we holding onto?

We have become slaves to our model. We always will if we have our eyes on the model we are creating.

DEFINE YOUR MODEL AS IT IS RIGHT NOW

Having just read the first six chapters, can you define where your church is right now? Are you a slave to the model you have? Can you define what part of the church you most identify with and why? Can you define your church without using WHERE or WHEN terminology? Can you define it "as He wants it to be" and take it somewhere other than where and when it is? Can you define it by using very little HOW and a lot of WHO and WHAT?

If I asked you "where" your church is, you would probably give me a city and a state. If I asked specifically, you would give me an address. I suggest that you think this way. Think of how many people regularly gather and call themselves church at that address. Can they call themselves church without just one address? Think about how many of those people also have a home address, a business address, an address for their school, an address where they shop for groceries, an address where they gas their car, an address for a haircut, an address of a hardware store they frequent, an address for the gym, an address for a favorite restaurant, an address for a car repair shop, an address for their favorite coffee shop, an address for the doctor's office, and an address for the dentist's office. I just laboriously listed 13 potential addresses. Let's assume the people of your church go to 10 of those per week. If you have 500 people in your church, then you have 5,000 church addresses that week. This does not even take into account your kids' or grandkids' soccer teams, sporting events, concerts, malls, emails, and online social networks. How many addresses do your people have? Are they at those addresses doing something important? Are they planting something there, or are they just like a leaf— hanging out at the end of a branch soaking up sunlight. Wasting 5,000 potential planting opportunities. Yes, I know. Leaves play a valuable role in the photosynthesis process. But trees which have leaves and yet do not produce fruit, Jesus kills. It is ALWAYS in season for spiritual fruit.

WHAT IF YOUR CHURCH WERE A TREE?

Trees grow out, not in. If your church were a tree, your people would be the branches. The fruit would be at the end of the branches. The fruit is the character of Christ which is supposed to produce disciples which are reproducible. Yet what we have mostly are the "leaves of attendance." Multiple leaves of attendance. We have very bushy trees. We measure leaves, which do not reproduce. If the branches are our people, then the limbs and trunks are our systems and programs that we as leaders oversee. What flows through is decided by the leadership. What do we tell people is expected and important? What do we say is a success? What if we started delivering Jesus through that system? What would it produce at the end? Fruit! Reproducible fruit! Leaves just fall off. Fruit reproduces.

Can they call themselves "church" without just one address?

Jesus had something to say about that. "Seeing a lone fig tree by the road, He came to it and found nothing on it except leaves only; and He said to it, 'No longer shall there ever be any fruit from you.' And at once the fig tree withered" (Matthew 21:19, NAS).

We are overly concerned with controlling and measuring. We have forgotten our job is to plant. If we do not plant, there will be no harvest to measure. If we were growing carrots, we would dig them up every day and measure them.

Do not hear me saying that I want you to become that person who is SO obnoxious about Jesus that they turn the planet off. I am just asking you to consider how many opportunities your church encounters in any given week.

The Tipping Point, by Malcolm Gladwell, is a good read to help you see "how little things can make a big difference."*

LEADERS MUST LEARN TO ASK TWO QUESTIONS

As leaders help release the people they serve to "relate and deliver the character of Christ", they must start by being willing to ask two questions. These two questions are about "releasing" people from within the HOW into their WHERE and WHEN. Here are the two questions:

1. What do you want to do for the King?
2. How can I help you?

Your job as a church leader is that simple. It is how you serve them. It is not about "containment" but "release." Can we teach them in such a way that they really do get the WHO-WHAT-WHY and then free people up to do the HOW-WHEN-WHERE? To minister in ways they see fit as guided by their King? Are there also cooperative ministries just waiting to be started? They just need permission and something to deliver AS THEY GO!

How do your layers stack up? Are they so thick that no one can truly see Jesus? Do people see the layers—the visuals—the symbols? Or are the layers invisible so that Christ is visible? Let's look at the two ways layers work. They are

---

* Malcolm Gladwell, *The Tipping Point: How Little Things Can Make a Big Difference* (New York: Back Bay Books, 2002).

either confining (containing) or permeable (releasing). They hold Him in or let Him out. Can people see through all that you have and say and do and really see Him? Or is there so much going on that, though it may be good in a small way, it is distracting and makes seeing Him cloudy at best?

YOU ARE FREE TO LIVE SENT

(Note: I did not coin the term "live sent." A friend named Jason Dukes did* Jason describes life as "living sent." As being the living letter Paul says we are. We are sent by Christ to all those we come in contact with. It is a great concept which helps us get out of the "Sunday only" thoughts when it comes to church.

"You show that you are a letter from Christ, the result of our ministry, written not with ink but with the Spirit of the living God, not on tablets of stone but on tablets of human hearts" (2 Corinthians 3:3).

If it is true that we are sent and we are living letters, the next question is: are you sent, or are you in a holding bin just sitting there going nowhere?

Most of the time we invite people to a place at a certain time. If we can learn to live sent, we can invite them to the person first.

---

* See: www.westpointchurch.org and www.JasonDukes.com.

DO YOUR LAYERS CONFINE?

I need to go back and spend a little more time on the WHO. You will encounter resistance in your own soul and in ways you never guessed existed. You are now playing around with somebody's religion. And that can be worse than politics.

Who—The WHO must be Jesus

Outside of the 6 layers are the people we say we are trying to reach. Are we BEING the church?

If we were growing carrots, we would dig them up every day and measure them.

Here are some abstract statements which are hard to understand. But think of them in terms of the layers of the earth diagram earlier.

It seems to me that we have put a lot of HOW in the middle. Even some WHERE and WHEN are in the middle of most church models.

Bill France came in 5th place in the first Daytona race in 1936. They had to stop the race three laps short.* In the 1911 Indianapolis 500, Ray Harroun started in 28th position, led 88 of the laps, took 6:42:08 to complete the race, and traveled at a mind-blowing 74.602 mph. And the track

---

* http://en.wikipedia.org/wiki/Bill_France,_Sr.

at the time was not asphalt; it was brick.* I do that on I-4 (in a 70 mph zone, of course). Has NASCAR and Indy evolved? Yes. But they are still about speed. They have not forgotten the core of what they are about. And at the same time, there are some odd rules they must follow that are designed by them. Both races have changed. They have added some layers. But they are still mainly about speed.

They have kept speed as their WHAT. Can we keep Jesus as our WHO?

Ask yourself:

1. WHAT do I really want? Can there be a WHO inside the WHAT?
2. Define the WHAT in terms that are minimal—size it all the way down to WHAT REALLY. Almost the QBQ, the "question behind the question" approach. Or the "statement behind the statement."
3. Boil till you get the basic essence of it.
4. Attempt to define your WHAT with no HOW.
5. Then, can your WHAT assume some other HOW?
6. Define your HOW with no required WHERE or WHEN.
7. We must be forced to define our WHAT with a relational paradigm. Or it is pure pragmatism.

---

* http://www2.indystar.com/cgi-bin/indy500/

8.   By doing these you will find your pure purpose. Then you can add some desired layers which will not hinder the WHO.

DISCUSSION GROUP

Make sure you have a computer so you can check out some of the websites. I still suggest you find two or more friends and discuss what you have read. And yes, I still think the best way to do that is for each of you to go back and highlight the five questions or statements that God used to impact you in this last chapter. Then get together, order something different, and sit and talk about why those words struck you and how God may be using them in your life. Two of these questions need to be the big ones in the middle: What do you want to do for the King? How can I help you? Can you go talk to your pastor, leader, or priest and tell that person what you think God may be asking you to do for Him?

You will see this same paragraph at the end of each chapter, because I think it is important to talk to others about what God is doing.

Chapter 8

Permeable Layers

L ET'S REVISIT THE WHO—JESUS. You can't spend too much time on Him. At His baptism, God spoke for the first time in over 400 years!! God broke His complete silence of 400 years when He said, "This is my Son, whom I love; with him I am well pleased" (Matthew 3:17). God did not chide the problems of the day. He did not chastise the layers of law and duty the Jewish leaders had put upon the people. He simply pointed to Jesus.

INDIVIDUALLY

How transparent are you? Are you clear? Can people see WHO is in you? Or do you have so many layers, problems, and masks, which cause your actions and attitudes to belie the fact that Christ actually lives in you, even though you speak of Him? My mask is humor. When I am not sure how to address a subject or a person, I insert humor. I have gotten very good at it over time. But it wastes precious moments with people who matter. Don't get me wrong, humor is OK. It just cannot be the main fare all the time.

What in you is keeping Jesus from being visible?

In the church of the recent past we have celebrated our layers. Not that getting people farther up the pyramid of leadership is all bad. Or we have circles and we want to get as many people farther into the circles as possible, which is not all bad. But it seems to me that we have done so much of that, that we have missed the core—Jesus. What about doing things backwards? What about Jesus BEING the core and then us pushing Jesus out toward them through the layers? The core should permeate the layers. The layers should not conceal the core. The core should be released through the layers. The layers should not "contain" (verb) the core. All the layers and everyone having anything to do with any of the layers should be pushing the core out. He should be obvious in everything we do; He should be the reason for everything we do. What if we were to give everyone we know something of value they could hand off? No matter who they are. No matter that they just came to Christ. No matter that they are one of the senior leaders in the church, or the senior pastor. If we made it basic enough that just about everyone could do it, and then applaud when they do—when they "be the church"—then more would do it. I think God applauds when we "be the church." A friend of mine once told me that in business it was not getting a few big bites. It was getting millions of little nibbles. So let's think about nibbling all day. Every day. All week long.

This chapter is just a few examples of what it means for Jesus to permeate out as opposed to Him being contained in a specific spot or a particular time. Remember it is more about release than it is containment.

Following are just some ways to think about it. We don't all understand things in the same way. So I have tried to put some odd examples or parallels to it.

INSIDE-OUT or OUTSIDE-IN?

Look at it this way. The traditional leadership goes from crowd to core. We train and train and set up hoops to jump through to get leaders into that inner circle. Then we celebrate who is in the inner circle. It is about what we pull in less than what we push out.

Jesus said that "he who is least among you all—he is the greatest" (Luke 9:48). How does that fit into this model? Jesus also had to listen to Momma Zebedee, with her two "sons of thunder," (and with names like that, couldn't they have asked for themselves?) requesting if they could sit on His right and left, when He came into His kingdom (Matthew 20:20ff). They knew they wanted to be next to Jesus. Once you know Him, who doesn't want to be close to Him? But their request was more about the power of the position than it was about living an influential life with Him as the center. You see, even though it is verse 20:20, she didn't see things very clearly. But before we go off on those three, we need to admit that we too think about position and powerful influence. We struggle to see 20:20.

The layers should not conceal the core.
The core should be released through the layers.

That is the reason we have things set up the way we do. They thought it was going to be an earthly kingdom soon. We attempt to set up a kingdom and call it church. The hierarchy is there. We can't deny it. Jesus responded to the two that the decision was up to His Father. They did not know that Jesus actually would live inside them soon and their desire to be close to Him would be fulfilled. However, it was not "sitting next to Him." It was "taking Him wherever they went." We too should just go about the business at hand. In other words, we all are to be about the basics. God will decide just who sits where when we are no longer in this current physical state. So it really is inside-out.

COMPUTING IN A CLOUD

Here is an odd illustration. In 2005, Mary Lou Jepson, a pioneering LCD screen designer, was asked to be the lead for a team, which was tasked to develop a laptop for $100. This laptop would become known as One Laptop Per Child (OLPC). Nicholas Negroponte, the MIT Media Lab visionary, wanted to get a laptop to every child in developing countries. What Jepson ended up doing turned the computer industry upside down.*

Jepson developed a laptop with only a flash drive (no hard drive to break if you drop it). It uses Linux operating system (free—open source). It has Wi-Fi and a color screen and full keyboard. And it uses the cloud of constant information

---

* Clive Thompson, "The Notebook Effect: How Cheap Little Laptops Hit the Big Time," *Wired Magazine*, 23 February 2009.

for all its needs. So, you go anywhere and you have what you need. It has become the favorite in Europe. The reason? Everyone could use it because it costs so little and is designed for constant connection.

Can we rethink church so that more people can get it? Can we be computers which move around constantly connected to the source and sharing that source with anyone who needs it? Can we get the layers of church bureaucracy diminished to the point that they are invisible and Christ is visible? Are we willing to pay the price to make Jesus visible and available?

LAMPS AND LIGHT

Try thinking of it this way. The church is a lamp, and all the people in it (as followers of Christ) are lamps (since the church IS people). By design, the purpose of a lamp is to shine light. If all you do as individual lamps is attempt to absorb light while you are "at" the church, you have missed your function. Lamps don't absorb anything. They give off something—light! However, if you view going "to church" to be with other believers and worship the One who gave you light in the first place, then gatherings become a place for battery recharging. And the great thing about battery recharging is that you can stay connected to the original light source and the battery charger all day, every day. He is always there for you. But your point is to shine all day, every day of every week.

How many bushel baskets does it take to put out one lamp? One, according to Mark 4:21ff. The baskets here represent layers over the light. The basket encases the light so that it is no longer visible. If we have WHEN baskets over our WHERE baskets over our HOW baskets over our WHY baskets over our WHAT baskets, we can't even see the WHO in the middle. He is the reason we supposedly do all that we do. All those looking on think the only time, place, or way they can see some light is when we decide they can. How confining. How impermeable.

So, do you thin layers, remove baskets, or just get everyone a cheap laptop? Well, the first two are feasible. When thinking through HOW you get Jesus to shine through everything you do collectively and individually, you may have to drop some of the ways you do things and adopt some new habits.

WHEN JESUS PUTS THE SQUEEZE ON YOU

Read Jeremiah 18:1–4. What is in should get out. God made you into a vessel which can contain something. He did not make you into a figurine. The vessel He makes us into contains Him. We are to pour Him out to a thirsty world. My wife inherited a few Hummels®, which were purchased by her grandmother in Germany. For the uninitiated, Hummels® are very fine clay figurines. I had no idea what they were when we got married. But they are quite sought-after collectibles. Though they are pretty, they have absolutely no use. I am not saying that you should not collect them. I am saying they have no other use but collection.

Ours collect dust in their cabinet. They are figurines, not vessels. My point here is this.

God intends on fashioning us in such a way that we are usable daily vessels of Him. What He puts in us, we are to give out. Rivers of living water should flow from us because He lives in us.

Question: Is the water visible to others? Or, are you and your church a collection of figurines? Pretty but not useful for the kingdom. God wants to reshape us for use in the kingdom. He was telling that to Israel then and He is telling it to us now. We are His property, His clay, and He should be allowed to shape us into any vessel He wants. When we resist and we become hardened in a particular shape, we become less useful when things change. Has "church" become so hardened into one shape that it is not as useful as it could be for the kingdom?

TUBULAR THEOLOGY

You got a bit of it in chapter five. Isaiah 55:10–11 is important. I missed it most of my life. His intent is that His word not come back void. No matter how many times I heard sermons on that, I still did not understand it. Not until I realized that verse 10 is the illustration for verse 11. Verse 10 is actually an explanation of what we now call the water cycle. Water (also in snow form) is sent from Heaven. Picture this. Water molecules evaporate over the Gulf of Mexico and collect as a cloud. They move inland over Tampa and head northeast. About 40 miles inland they are dropped as rain.

They soak into the ground then into the root system of an orange tree. The tree then uses the water molecule to help produce an orange. The orange is picked, goes to the market and is purchased. It is then taken home and eaten two days later. The person eating the orange happens to be a jogger. Later that day the molecule makes its way to a sweat gland on the joggers' forehead and then evaporates and goes back up to the clouds. I know this is not a technical description of the water cycle, but it works here. In this illustration, the orange is what nourishes, and the seeds can then grow another orange tree.

God intends His word to travel the same path. His word comes from Him, gives us nourishment and something for us to give away. The person receiving what we have to give would then maybe attempt to thank us for what we have given. We need to say thanks but remind them that all good and perfect gifts come from God. We then encourage them to thank God for the gift. When they do, His word has now made the cycle. Not the water cycle, but the word cycle.

Do the systems and programs or your church encourage giving away what we have so that He can be visible?

PRUNING OR TOPIARY?

In John 15:2 Jesus speaks of His Father being a gardener. "Every branch in Me that does not bear fruit, He takes away; and every branch that bears fruit, He prunes it so that it may bear more fruit" (NAS). When God prunes us, He does so in order that we might produce more fruit. He never trims us so we will achieve a certain shape. A topiary is a shaped bush. A good example is at Disney World. They trim it into the shape of Mickey Mouse. It stays in one shape for its whole life—the shape of Mickey Mouse. God has no desire for you to become a spiritual topiary and grace some church lawn. He is not interested in ornamental Christians. We assume too often that He has a shape in mind for us—then He trims us into that shape. Not true. Even though He has work planned for us to do (Ephesians 2:10), He is pruning us for more growth. He has one shape in mind, one image: His Son. And we have to change daily for that image to shine through. It is not a static existence.

As leaders, do we hinder God in His pruning? Are we simply attempting to produce Christian topiaries? As we struggle to make disciples, are we lopping off what doesn't look like what WE think they should look like? Do we have so many preconceived notions of what a mature believer looks like that we are actually thwarting God in His work on that person for pruning? Are we trimming so much that fruit is never allowed to develop? Are we aiming for topiaries?

As you go through your day, think about this: Do you see the potential for growth that God sees in the people you know? Do you then assist in the pruning to help them grow to that potential? Are you "releasing" them in a fruitful way, or "containing" them for a certain shape?

COMFORT AS A FREE GIFT

Read 2 Corinthians 1:3-4: "Blessed be the God and Father of our Lord Jesus Christ, the Father of mercies and God of all comfort, who comforts us in all our affliction so that we will be able to comfort those who are in any affliction with the comfort with which we ourselves are comforted by God" (NAS). Say that three times fast! What do you think the operative word is? My guess is "comfort." So, what we get from God in the form of comfort should be given to those who need comfort. Do the layers of your church allow for that? Is it encouraged? Is it expected? Does what you do in church have a time where comfort can be a part of it? Does your life exhibit comfort?

Too much of the time we tend to forget that life and church life are to be about making Him (and His attributes) visible. Yet we spend a lot of our time attempting other things. All our days need to be about giving His attributes away. He will fill us up to the degree we give Him away.

The layers should let Him out—not hold Him in.

DISCUSSION GROUP

This week your meal out will be "potluck" or "covered dish." Or, if it is a group of single guys, "drive-through." The reason is that this week should represent the many ways things can be illustrated. And yes, I still think the best way to do that is for each of you to go back and highlight the five questions or statements that God used to impact you in this last chapter. Then get together, and sit and talk about why those words struck you and how God may be using them in your life. What illustrations can you come up with which represent making the layers of church "thin" so people can see Jesus?

You will see this same paragraph at the end of each chapter, because I think it is important to talk to others about what God is doing.

Chapter 9

The Elephant:
How-Where-When

Y OU PROBABLY THINK THIS would be a large chapter since I am talking about the proverbial elephant in the room. It is not. Everybody knows when there is an elephant in the room. Nobody wants to talk about it. We ignore its existence. But sometimes it is so large it crowds out everything which SHOULD be in the room.

INDIVIDUALLY

What is your elephant? What do you not want to talk about? My wife and I used to play a game. When we knew we had time on our hands, driving or whatever, one of us would make the statement, "Tell me something you do not want to tell me." Now you had to be ready because you, in turn, had to be willing to answer the same question.

Made us be more open about the things that really needed to be discussed so we could move toward an ever-growing love relationship.

I have another question I have told most my leadership in the past that I would ask of them and they could ask of me at any time. Here it is: "If I saw something in your life I thought you would want to know, would you want me to tell you about it?"

That will get the elephants exposed. How ready are you to discuss what really needs to be discussed?

I don't know your elephant, so this is not a "HOW-to" book. It is a HOW-to-HOW book. The intent is not to show you the elephant—your current How-Where-When. It is to get you thinking through the Who-What-Why's in such a way that it challenges your thinking processes (next chapter) and encourages you in the directions God asks YOU to go. How you do what you do is up to you and God. Then you are to figure it out where you are—your city, your county, your country, rural or very urban.

The elephant will not leave the room whole. You must take him apart piece by piece through discussions about him. But if you never talk about him being in there, you will never really discuss him and disassemble him and extract him from the premises. You know your elephant. Only you can take him apart.

For many of us, our HOW, instead of Jesus, has been at the core. Church system has been used as methods of pragmatism and we have used Jesus to accomplish our HOW. Wonder what He thinks about that?

HOW—Here you need to spend a lot of time thinking through the facts of your case. But get ready. Almost everyone in your church will probably agree on the WHO-WHAT-WHEN. You will probably find quite a bit of resistance in the

HOW. But, you are probably ALREADY experiencing frustrations. So, why not experience the ones that lead toward growth in Christ, not the death rattles of a system? USE the systems to inject a new DNA of Who-What-Why. Can we take the current systems and structures and line them up in such a fashion, using the worship/discipleship/stewardship model, that we need less of the HOW-WHERE-WHEN? Can we help people slow down long enough to stop? Then really think about "what" we are doing?

In reSymboling, the HOW, you must take into consideration many cultural facts. Where you are on the planet will define how you are able to work through this. Will you structure your discipleship as a mentor-based program? Will you utilize the home cell system? Will you try to tackle the G-12 reproducing model every 18 months? Will you tweak an old Sunday school model?

The elephant will not leave the room whole.

In worship gatherings, will you stay with a structured "everybody knows" what is going to happen next because they have it in print? Will you be too unstructured for people to have a sense of direction? They just feel good to have been in the moment. When "stewarding" your property and finances, how much will you give way? How much will you spend on yourselves? How much do you think needs to be spent on staff; on buildings and maintenance; on sending short-term missionaries? How much will you spend on local ministries? How much to para-church organizations?

How will you carry this out so that Jesus Christ is obviously and visibly the center and reason for it all?

WHERE

Have we overcommitted ourselves to the WHERE (one spot on the planet) and think that everything needs to happen there and we need to be "at the church house" all the time? I am not saying not to use your buildings. Maybe you can just use them for another group of people? Ask yourself, "Who do we know that could use our building?" Then ask, "Could this be a way to care for the community in which we live?" Most church buildings sit empty most of the time. If you can get past that fact that the buildings are not the church (you are the church) and they are just buildings, then you can possibly rethink their use.

I am not saying here that we use our property less. We just need to use it less for US who are already there. Use the buildings for the sake of the community. Exercise your spot, your normal WHERE you do what you do for a reason other than yourself. Think about this. How many church plants have you heard of that rent public schools to use on Sunday for worship gathering? Why not use the Sunday school space you have for a charter school? Why not let a public school utilize your space when they need to have a major remodel of one of their buildings? Why not say to your city government, since there is overcrowding in the public schools, we will let you use our buildings until we can come up with a solution that doesn't just tax the citizens to death?

This is taking stewardship from Chapter 5 and using the WHERE that you own (your buildings) in a relational way. Use your things to love the community. Is it starting to sink in? Use what you have for others. Don't think what you have (buildings) is where you always have to be. To the degree that we only use it for us, we are truly being selfish.

How will you define the WHERE and use what you have so that Jesus Christ is obviously and visibly the center and reason for it all?

WHEN

Get a group of your spiritually sharp business leaders together and ask them this question: "How many of you would start a business, build buildings, and then utilize them less than 5% of the hours in a week?" I think I know their answer. If someone wanted to start a Starbucks franchise but told Starbucks Corporate that they were only planning to be open for 6 hours a week, corporate would not even entertain a discussion with them. Yet that is what we seem to do a lot of the time. The WHERE and the WHEN seem to always be together.

The volume of time the buildings sit there empty is 165 hours a week. So the WHEN can we utilize them is 165 more hours a week. The volume of time they are basically empty is 95%. Can you figure ways to utilize them not just for yourselves but for the community? How can you steward them in a more positive way? Now can you help your people to use their 165 hours (WHEN they are not at the church buildings) for the sake of Jesus and His kingdom?

When you do what you do, how can you make certain that Jesus Christ is obviously and visibly the center and reason for it all? Do you see a theme here? Is Christ central? If HOW and WHERE and WHEN (and even WHAT and WHY) overshadow Him, then some of the WHAT-WHY-HOW-WHERE-WHEN has migrated to the center—where He should be.

IS IT REALLY POSSIBLE?

We tell Jesus we want to work on His behalf, but it generally has to happen in a very specific way (how), in a particular building (where), at a certain time (when). We have put HOW constraints on the gospel, WHERE constraints on the gospel and WHEN constraints on the gospel.

The big question is this: Is the daily flow of character important enough for us to reSymbol what we do and how we do it? Can we focus on the three areas that Christ himself focused on and was involved in daily? His connection with the Father (worship) flowed into every moment of His life. Many of those moments He spent helping and teaching people about who His Father is (discipleship) and He was constantly aware that He be a good steward of what His Father had given Him. He did all that the Father asked Him to do with what and who He was given (John 17). He used what He had for the sake of others and kept nothing for

Himself. He used Himself for us to the point of death. It is your turn to prove to the world who He is. Are you up to the task?

The early church mimicked that daily lifestyle very well in Acts 2:42. Can we? They showed us it IS possible even in a crumby society with an incredibly tough Roman environment.

To do this we need to ask three questions:

- How are we encouraging worship all day, every day?
- How are we encouraging discipleship all day, every day?
- How are we encouraging stewardship all day, every day?

Is the daily flow of character important enough for us to reSymbol what we do and how we do it?

When I talk about this, people often wonder if it can be that simple. The early church was able to accomplish it 2,000 years ago in a society much worse and corrupt than our own. It is happening today around the globe. Is it happening with you?

So let me interrupt you with the fact that it has been proven that those three things can be done.

WHICH ONE ARE YOU?

Are you getting it done or being interrupted? I know that the book *Simple Church* has helped a lot of people.* And for that I am grateful. Sometimes less is more. Sometimes we spend so much time organizing our How-Where-When that we confuse even ourselves about the reason we exist.

Right about now you are saying to yourself, "If I do all that I have thought about doing, if I change all that I am thinking of changing, and if I start all that I am thinking about starting this may kill me or my church." That is probably true. But let me say two things here. One, you do not need to do all of it today. Even God took six days to create the universe. And two, you and your church may be dying anyway. All you will be doing is hastening the death. Yes that seems callous. But if there is one bit of life left in your church, one bit of remnant, wouldn't you want to fan that flame till it is ablaze again? Or wouldn't you want to get out of the way so that some other part of the kingdom can use your property/resources to flourish? Again, yes that seems harsh. But this whole church thing has been too personalized by the West. It is "Thy kingdom come" we pray in the Lord's Prayer. Do we really mean it? Or is it "My kingdom come?" Do we really want His kingdom to come? Do we want to be a part of it? Or do we want to stand in the way? Do we want His kingdom to come, but in our way?

---

* Thom S. Rainer and Eric Geiger, *Simple Church: Returning to God's Process for Making Disciples* (Nashville: B&H Books, 2006).

The world is moving so fast these days that the man who says it can't be done is generally interrupted by someone doing it.

—Elbert Hubbard

Stop and pray. Ask God to reveal what is next for you to do. He will use you in ways you cannot even imagine.

DISCUSSION GROUP

This week, eat elephant. Just figuratively. This week discuss things that may not be safe to discuss—the elephant. Use those statements that God used to impact you in this last chapter. Then get together, and sit and talk about why those words struck you and how God may be using them in your life.

You will see this same paragraph at the end of each chapter, because I think it is important to talk to others about what God is doing.

Chapter 10

Your Dad Is a Genius

WHAT IS THE MOST expensive piece of real estate on the planet? Give up? A grave. Because there are so many ideas buried there. What ideas will they bury with you? What are you personally holding on to which God wants you to give away? How often do you "not" believe in yourself? When you do not believe what God says is true? He is a genius and gives great thoughts and ideas to His children.

No matter where you are, who you are, or what condition your life or your church is in, His Spirit can lead you into new ways of thinking and doing what He asks. You have to be willing. Are you?

> Imagination is more important than knowledge.
> —Albert Einstein

Einstein understood that your mind is a terrible thing to waste. Your Heavenly Father is a creator. The biggest creator ever! He is your Abba Father. His DNA is in you. You are no longer boxed up. Drop the crate and create! But that is not as easy as just deciding and starting. Though our hearts may be turned toward God and we are ready to live beyond where we are. There are many default settings in your mind. They need to be opened to thinking differently than you have thought before. This chapter is designed to start rewiring some of your thought processes. You need to think beyond where and how you have thought. Otherwise you will come up with the same answers. Those answers are not working now.

We cannot solve our problems with the same thinking we used when we created them. Albert Einstein

---

Einstein also knew that our tendency is to allow the default settings to rule. Is it possible that your default settings may have some inconsistencies or incorrectness?

So let's start. Can you be honest about these two spiritual truths?

One: What you know of God and the workings of His kingdom is not ALL there is to know.

Two: Some of what you do know of God, and are convinced of, is WRONG.

When you have conceded on those two statements, you may be able to hear Him as He speaks. You may be able to think beyond where you have thought in the past. He may have been whispering to you for some time about a new way of doing something important to Him, but you could not hear Him because the default setting kept getting in the way. First, you must say, "I was wrong; I am sorry. Can you forgive me? Can we start fresh?" WOW, how hard is that going to be!

Can you be creative in coming up with new ways to do the same things? Or new things? Can you stop the thinking of the past and start using some new thinking for the future?

If staff and leaders are willing to do this, then we can involve the whole church and every pew or seat or cushion and start redefining the ideology or the HOW. It can become a cure for the common church.

Once we figure out how to make Jesus available for everyone to share (and not keep Him layered up), we can start thinking of new ways to care. New ministries to start. Not ones that just the "church" runs, but ministries that happen daily in the lives of all those who share our Lord. When God gives a few people the same idea and they get together, who knows what can happen. Celebrate Recovery* was the idea of a lay person at Saddleback Community Church. They went with it. Now it is a huge ministry changing millions of lives.

If we want different answers, we must ask different questions. Our problem is that we always ask the same questions: How can I grow my Sunday school? How can I increase attendance in the worship service? What if we started asking, "How can I help you in your daily life so you can be impactful?" I think the church systems we have all created or inherited have engineered creativity out of us. Can we reclaim it?

---

* Celebrate Recovery is a Christ-centered recovery program for all types of habits, hurts, and hang-ups. (www.celebraterecovery.com)

We have bought into the belief that God and His wonder can be found on Sunday in a worship "Service" and in a prearranged classroom setting for Sunday School. Though those are not all bad, they are just not all there is. But once we do that long enough, it is all we know to do. We have built these buildings that are used for the Sunday three hours and maybe another three hours a week some other time. Once we have done that long enough, our egos kick in and we move into the comparison mode. In some places it seems like we have erected a modern-day Tower of Babel. And God is now confusing our language because He does not want us building any longer. He wants to shift our attention.

INDIVIDUALLY

Again, I am not saying that we ditch the current systems. Remember, they are like the trunk and major limbs of that tree. Yet the tree is producing only leaves...no fruit...nothing reproducible. We must use the systems (trunk/limbs: worship service/Sunday School) to inject the new DNA of relational connection all week long. So that we can again start to see fruit.

The question becomes: What do we expect of the people we serve all week long? Can we be creative enough to come up with new ways to encourage it, show it, and celebrate it?

By NOT comparing, Frankensteining, or squeezing the bride, we are free to take apart all of our symbols and discard or realign them within the answers of these three questions.

We must deconstruct carefully. If we do not, we will look as though we are committing spiritual euthanasia.

In the movie *A Knights Tale*, Edward, the Prince of Wales, knights William Thatcher after releasing him from the stockades. Edward states his historians have discovered that William is from an ancient line of forgotten knights. He states that William is a knight and that Edward as Prince, having said that, it is incontestable.

You are incontestably HIS. You are released and free to serve the King in His kingdom.

Again I ask the question, "What is stopping you?"

THE JESUS STORY

The Trinity was having a discussion in Heaven one day. God the Father was wondering why He saw so many churches in America that were not having any impact on the society He put them in. So He asked Jesus to take a clipboard and go down there and see. He checked on many churches without them knowing He was there. Upon His return to Heaven, He handed God the report. He noted, "They seem to love each other enough. They tend to spend a little too much money and time on buildings they only use five or six hours a week. The other 160+ hours of their week, they tend to spend on themselves. And I did check: every one of them has enough widows near them to make sure they are taken care of. There are lots of single parents and kids who are orphaned too. Each church is strategically planted with a poor section of town within driving distance. And I have noticed that each member has people in each of their lives who have needs. Some of the older ones need help around the house and for someone to talk to them. Each of the businessmen has friends who really need to be open about their struggles. The teenagers have lots of friends who just need someone to be nice to them. They seem to really pick at one another. So, Father, I have given them all they need to be successful. It must be a heart issue. I think they have forgotten how to live in their own lives. You had better send the Holy Spirit to see what He can do."

What is stopping you?

As you start again to freely live as though you were "sent," you will be answering the two "Dream Builders Network" questions:

- Who do you want to help?
- How do you want to help them?*

You are taking Christ with you as you go! The seed is being planted!!!!

Never leave these two questions. The church is a WHO, not a WHAT or a WHERE. The people who are a part of your church and those who are not a part of your church are people.

---

* See: www.DreamBuildersNetwork.org.

Can we think creatively enough to move beyond yesterday? If we are related to The Creator, why are our brains stuck thinking thoughts we have always thought? And why are we doing what we have always done?

EVANGELISM EXERCISE

Why not actually do some reSymboling with just one word in one area of your church? We will begin to chart your path. Let's start with one word. That word is Evangelism. In conference settings, I use this exercise. I write the word Evangelism on a whiteboard and then write speed thoughts from the audience. The whiteboard is filled up with words and statements that come to mind when they think of the word evangelism (www.ReleasingChurches.org).

We will find out how it fits within the three questions and what changes in thoughts occur about it. We'll also notice expectations concerning it. Most of the time people come up with generally the same answers. Then I set aside that whiteboard for a few moments. We'll come back to this in a moment.

Can we think creatively enough to move beyond yesterday?

I then do another exercise. I say, "How well do we live free? How well do we actually hear God's voice during a normal week? Let's see how well you can hear my voice."

Each participant has a blank sheet of copier paper, and I say this:

I am going to say two things...

1.

2.

You have two minutes...go.

(See: www.ReleasingChurches.org; on the web, we have YouTube videos of the two statements.)

I then ask: "Who invented flight?" Most of the time people say the Wright brothers. When actually it was God. The Wrights discovered manned flight.

Too much of the time we hear things which are not said and answer questions that were not asked.

There are several important lessons we can take away from this exercise...in asking "What is God saying?":

"MISSING ONE WORD CAN CAUSE MAJOR FAILURE"

"Hearing what is not said can cause failure."

- You must learn to listen closely to hear Him.
- Change is unavoidable. Make sure it is a "God's change."
- Do not run off to completion. Our mental default settings.
- If you plan to color outside the lines, you must have new crayons (new symbols).

We need new ways of thinking about what is successful. If you plan to be outside the box and draw outside the box, you will need new ways of measuring success. But those new ways must be held lightly in your hand. Remember, no squeezing of the bride.

We need to retrain our mind and our heart to what we are about.

Exercise for reSymboling

Here is another exercise I like to use to see if our brains can re-think something. Turn the Roman numeral XI into the number 6. You may draw one line.

Try it again. Turn the Roman numeral XI into the number 6. But you can't use what I just showed you.

Try it one more time. Turn the Roman numeral XI into the number 6. This time you are not allowed to draw on your paper.

This exercise helps us see just how hard it is to think beyond where we have thought.

On the first try you could have turned your paper over and written a capital S in front of the I. It then becomes the word SIX.

The second one requires that you put the number 6 before the X then an = sign and a 6 after the I. It is now a multiplication problem which expresses 6.

The third time, turn the paper over and fold it across the middle of the X and the I. Then unfold it halfway. It becomes VI on one side of the fold with a "reflection" of VI on the other side of the fold. IT really IS possible to look at something from different angles if you will work at it long enough.

(See: www.ReleasingChurches.com)

Missing one word can cause major failure

I saw Margaret Slusher do the first two in a Leadership Network conference. The third one I added. Can you creatively think of even more ways or other examples of thinking beyond where our mind normally takes us?

There are many ways to do the same thing and achieve successful results.

The big question is could you, armed with only the tubular diagrams and the two Dream Builder Network questions, redesign your church life without comparing and without frankensteining it? Can you create as He did? Do you hear Him saying again, "Let there be..."? This is going to require redefining church for some of these local expressions. It is going to require a shift from church as a WHAT to a WHO. The WHAT is only to give basis for thought for the WHY and HOW you get the WHO out. It is going to require a serious commitment from leaders to do life with these church families for the long haul. It is going to require a shift from "gathering" to "living sent." To be free to make it up as we go.

Will you set up some Dream Builders Network groups? It is only one way to release your people to hear God and go do as He asks.*

Creativity Mythbeliefs

- Creativity is reserved for smart people
- Kids are the only ones who are creative
- I am not creative
- Creativity happens only now and then
- Only those who were good in art, pottery, and band class are creative

The world is but a canvas to our imaginations.
—Henry David Thoreau

Yet, we are related to a creator!!

GOOD NEWS EXERCISE

Let's shift to new words. What is "good news"? (See the video at www.ReleasingChurches.org.) Again in conference settings, I use the exercise. I write the words good news on a white-board and then write speed thoughts from the audience. Again the whiteboard gets filled with words and statements that come to mind when they think of the words good news. No, I'll not divulge why I do this until later. You know, trade secrets.

---

* See: www.DreamBuildersNetwork.org.

The big question: Can you take what you learned and reSymbol using the relational triangle? Can you look at all that you say and do and put a new grid within it that says, "living relationally day by day with more and more of the character of Christ being a part of your life is the MOST important thing"?

Then use your system and programs to deliver the training. But do not expect that to be the only time you talk about it or DO IT!

THE MAIN THINGS

Don't let the main things get overshadowed by the system which is supposed to put forth the main things. Let me say it in a different way: Discipleship systems never make disciples. Disciples make disciples. Worshippers worship, and stewards steward. We are to be all three. But is that what we tell our people?

If we can see straight enough to focus on creating disciples, worshippers, and stewards out of the people He sends us, then He can guide them into where and how they are to carry out the loving of people in their lives. But there are things that will shut down our new creative thoughts.

> Imagination is the beginning of creation.
> —George Bernard Shaw

Regarding the two whiteboard experiences. You will note (if you watched the videos) that when I asked the question concerning evangelism, the answers were typical and had to do with structure, program, events, particular times, and particular ways. When I asked the questions about good news, I got answers that had to do more with character, relationship, and Jesus as a person.

Did you know that the word for evangelism is not even in the Bible? The word for evangelist is in there twice. The word meaning "telling good news" is in there 55 times. And not just telling it is Christ's meaning, but BEING it. He not only told good news; He WAS good news.

My point in the two whiteboard experiences is this: God is conforming us into the image of Christ. We are to be walking examples of Who He is. "As we go" the way we act and how we treat people tells them Who He is (good or bad). Someone in the cubicle next to you at work is watching you. And you used to be a jerk. But now you are a believer in WHO Jesus is; you are changing into His character. You are not as much of a jerk anymore. That is good news to the person in the cubicle next to you. You have just done evangelism without preaching it. 1 Peter 3:15 says, "But in your hearts set apart Christ as Lord. Always be prepared to give an answer to everyone who asks you to give the reason for the hope [the reason for change] that you have. But do this with *gentleness and respect*" (italics mine). All of this in a relational form is discipleship. Teaching others about Who Jesus is by our words and deeds. If there is no hope to be seen, then they never have a reason to ask a question about it. So now you see why the word for disciples is in the Bible 270 times and means "learner." So, "as you grow" and "as you go" are others learning (and are you then intentionally telling them) WHO Jesus is?

Isn't it incredible how God creatively put all this together and made it so simple? Isn't it also incredible how messed up and layered we have made it? Can you un-layer or make the layers as invisible as possible so the main point, Jesus, can be seen? You will have to get creative for that to happen.

DISCUSSION GROUP

This week, be intentionally creative in what and how you eat. It is still food and it is still eating. Be creative. Then find five questions and statements that God used to impact you in this last chapter. Then get together, and sit and talk about why those words struck you and how God may be using them in your life.

You will see this same paragraph at the end of each chapter, because I think it is important to talk to others about what God is doing.

Chapter 11

Questions Leaders Should Ask

I KNOW IT SAYS, "LEADERS." You may be one or you may be one in the making. At some point in some way everyone is a leader. Someone is watching what you say and do and is basing something on that. You are leading. Which way are you leading? The graph of questions at the end is by no means the end all of questions—just a starting point to get you going in a direction. As a person before God, can you ask yourself those questions and give honest answers? If you do, you will find that He is ready and willing to help you accomplish His will for your life.

INDIVIDUALLY

Leaders should ask more questions than they give answers. No one person has the market cornered on how we do what we do. Only God can say, "I Am Who I Am" as a declarative statement. And what He says goes. We all need to work with others to decide the answers to these questions. If we live in community, there is no dictator. So, everyone can play a part. It is the way He wants it. Otherwise I don't think He would have spent so much time in the New Testament telling us how to live together, in love together.

Having just about beaten the six questions to death, I still think we need to question things. It is so easy to become static and stale. Once you start thinking more and more about how you can get Jesus to shine through the layers, you need to consistently look for new ways of thinking about it. God does not want us to quit reSymboling just because we went through reSymbol. It is a continual process that we work until He comes back for us. It's not over until it's over. And if you are still reading this book, it is not over. Here are a few more questions and some restated ones to ponder:

- Can we do less policing and more releasing?
- Can you define success without using numbers or counting?
- Can you define success without using the words "more" or "most"?
- If you lost all of your church buildings and you were not allowed to rebuild, could you do church?
- What is the purpose of the pastoral staff?
- Could congregants have bigger dreams than the staff?
- Who gets to define which dream gets built?
- What are the limiting factors we may have unconsciously put on ourselves?

- Are you asking those gathered to do God's work in your ways?
- When gathering people, how do you define when "enough gathering is enough"?
- Are we willing to redefine "what works"?
- Is it more important that Christ be known or that we have our preference in church polity/structure?
- How can I (as a pastor) release all those folks out there into the kingdom for His sake?
- Should I (as pastor) be measuring "what" and "how" they are doing?
- Do I have to measure everything?
- What do they want to do that has not come to their minds because they know that the answer from the leadership is NO?
- Do they think I (as pastor) have all the ideas?
- Am I willing to consistently reSymbol?

RESYMBOL YOUR THOUGHT PROCESSES

Nowhere in the book did I say it would be easy. Some parts are less hard than others. Kingdom work has many obstacles stacked up against it. We need to push through and start seeing people more and more as He does. If you do, you will start being willing to fight through any of the questions above or the grid below. He will reprogram your thought processes. The following is just an attempt at working you through a process of thinking so that you can see how needs/causes get "stuck in the process" and many times never get taken care of. You may have a better list or adapt this one. But start reSymboling your thoughts to focus on people NOW.

(NOTE: This section is for AFTER you have decided and implemented a way of making as certain as possible that those you are "sending" daily understand the whole "character flow" issue and are immersed in that as their base purpose.)

Below is just a chart of questions you need to ask, making sure that you constantly answer them "as you go." Also, I am not suggesting that you stop helping make Sunday work. But that is only about three hours. These thoughts are designed to use the three and get us out into the other 165 hours. Your first answer could be a small one-time need or a large multi-layered need. Or it could be something you see which you will need lots of help with. Start asking Him to help you see the world and people as He does. When you are becoming who He wants you to be, as a loving disciple of His, then you need to make sure you do what it is He is asking you to do. Let nothing stop you, especially other people's opinions.

> The man with a new idea is a crank until the idea succeeds.
>
> —Mark Twain

You may need to spend a lot of time looking at and thinking about what it is you sense Him whispering in your ear. Narrowing things down to manageable ideas is always tough.

Creativity consists of coming up with many ideas, not just that one great idea.

— Charles Thompson

Step 1: Define the "as you go" need. (You have the WHO, this step is your WHAT)	
(Twenty-five words or less. Can't be about you or your church)	What do you want to do for the King?
	What does He want you to do for others?
	What and How do you think He wants you to do it?
Step 2: Re-focusing the WHAT on the WHO.	
What am I being asked by Him?	Does it fit Worship, Discipleship, or Stewardship?
What is the real opportunity?	Define the specifics. Cup of cold water?
How can I make sure it is part of the relational paradigm? How does red tape affect it?	Can you help them fix it long term so they can do unto others?
	Whose relational responsibility is it? Mine? Can I involve others?
Don't forget: we all do all three all the time.	Is the system limiting or confining?
Step 3: WHY should I do this?	
Never quit asking this. It forces you to make sure it is not about you.	Answer this question starting your sentence with "So that....", or "In order that...." Do not use "because..." or "Why not?"

Step 4: This is the HOW, WHERE, and WHEN	
How do I get the money I need to do it?	I can't afford to help them.
How can I get so and so to help me? ...or do I? Is someone's attitude blocking you?	I can't get past "so and so."
How do I get past my fear?	I could never do that for someone.
How do I get past my lack of knowledge?	Do I need to know something new to do this?
How do I gain the skill to do it? Do I need more skills, or do I just need to start?	What is stopping you? Why?
When can I schedule this?	Will you know someone else to help you get started? Is someone else doing this already?
When can I learn to do this - education?	Will you do it later? Can you ask someone else to help?
When will I solidify my commitment to it?	Will you be committed even if no one else will?
When are the results celebrated?	People need reminded regularly what God is doing.
When will my attitude change?	Can your attitude change to be more willing to GO?
Where will this be done?	The place needs to be decided.
Step 5: What past patterns have not worked? (In case you are stuck in a past pattern)	
List your top answers, then quit it...repeat this process until you have a list of ideas you have not tried.	If God has called you to help, He will show you a way.

Step 6: Redefine the WHY this needs done. (In case you get stuck—do this, then go back to #1)	
Define a simpler version of the opportunity.	Can you attack the reasons one by one?
Step 7: Reasons you need to seize this opportunity.	
What good will come from fulfilling this opportunity?	A person's life is changed. How?
Step 8: So what?	
What will happen if you find there is no solution? If you are compelled by Him, keep looking!	God will not be known by them.
Step 9: Reframe the opportunity.	
Shrink or expand the opportunity to encourage action.	Can you attack it from another angle?
Step 10: Is the compelling reason asked by God?	
YES!	
Step 11: Opportunity Definition	
	Eliminate barriers to static love.

This is not meant to be a comprehensive list. It is meant to be a beginning point for you to examine your motives. From time to time we all need to ask ourselves some tough questions. I hope and pray you do . . . for His sake.

DISCUSSION GROUP

A chapter about leadership questions is tough. If you are not a leader in your church, do you want the leaders to ask some of these questions? Do you want them to ask you what you think? Are you all together asking what God wants? Find five questions and statements that God used to impact you in this chapter and talk about what God may be up to.

You will see this same paragraph at the end of each chapter, because I think it is important to talk to others about what God is doing.

Chapter 12

The Baton Pass

W ELL, YOU MADE IT. The last chapter. Actually it is the first. Because now you have to decide if you are actually going to do some of what God put on your mind in the last eleven chapters. This is not a bait and switch. It is catch and release. You are caught by Him. He has breathed life in you through Christ. Now you are guided by His Holy Spirit to be all that He has made you to be. That means you must change.

INDIVIDUALLY

The baton pass is not just between generations, as I will speak of in a moment. It is about handing off Christ to anyone you meet. The pass will look different to you than you have seen in the past. But don't be shy. Get in the race.

We are living in interesting times. The "overlap," I like to call it. The last breaths of past systems and the first breaths of new freedom. We are all breathing it. Which breath do you relish? Can you, the older generations, allow the next generations of new believers to create the church of the future? Can you, the next generations, see the values of the older generations who hold Christ high? You might be surprised to know that the next generation has many who know their theology well and have just decided to "be the church" and "do church" differently than the established churches. And to the new generations, you might be surprised to see the dedication of the older generations to Christ and to one another, if you looked closely enough.

We spend too much time looking at and condemning the package. The visual. What we see.

We might not want the methods and buildings (or lack) of others to encumber the Word of God. Can't we find a way to utilize what we all have for the whole kingdom? I understand the zealous ideals of both groups. But I see the value in the established churches (and some of their buildings) being a prayer base, a sending point, a place to nurture new ministries, and a way of ensuring we get the most out of what He has given us.

THIS WILL REQUIRE A RELATIONAL THEOLOGY

What I've simply outlined in this book is a relational clothesline on which you can hang your practices. The practical must be relational or it will miss the mark. The theology is already in the Bible. God's point was relational. How have we missed it? "I have given them the glory that you gave me, that they may be one as we are one" (John 17:22). That is not a spatial closeness statement. That is a we-are-here-for-each-other relational statement. I have found a great place for relational theology and some literature to go with it: www.GreatCommandment.net.

Dr. David Ferguson and his team have been gifted by God to explain His word from a relational, not structural, standpoint. The WHO at the core is a person who desires being known, not just understood. If the baton the established generation attempts to hand off is a set of rules or a system, there are very few in the next generation who want that baton. If, however, your system contains a fresh set of relational paradigms which are missional, it is something the next generations may want to be involved in.

We know that God is relational and that He has freed us. Yet, we attempt to put ourselves and others right back in a box. Nobody wants somebody to hand them an empty container.

PERMISSIONISM AND CREDENTIALISM

These two things stand in the way of Christ many times. Permission is important if you are under authority. But never forget that you are always under Christ's authority. If His desire for your life requires you take up your cross and serve in a way different than you have permission, then you have a dilemma. Whom do you obey? If you remain under earthly authority, you must obey the earthly authority He has placed you under until you are released. However, if He requires you change your allegiance, He may be the authority you listen to and follow. Do not disobey your earthly authority. But exercise your right to follow Jesus where He leads. Never seek to be under no earthly authority at all. William Wilberforce understood this, and he used the authorities over him. He was the major force in abolishing slavery in England. Those of us who serve people should be accountable and responsible before Christ and them. As leaders, we should be giving more permission for our people to follow the lead of Christ instead of suggesting they follow us. They can do both. Paul did. But the Pauls of this world are rare.

The WHO at the core is a person who desires being known, not just understood.

Credentials are odd things. Some people have many credentials, but they may not fit their position. Some people fit their position but have few credentials. God may call you into something for which you have no credentials. At one time Peter had no credentials except that of a fisherman. As Jesus led him, he gained credence…credentials. Too much of the time we see a title and the seeming credentials that go with that title; we assume that they match. We then say to ourselves, "I could never be that person." We wrongly assume that God even wants us to be that person. He has called you to be you. Your credence comes from Christ. In time He will give you the credence you need to serve the people He calls you to.

As leaders, do you hold back permission from your people? Do you hold credentials or position over their heads? Jesus did neither. Follow Jesus and you will have (and give) permission and credentials. In Matthew 21:23ff Jesus is asked where His authority comes from. He was being asked by religious leaders and those in positions of authority. Of course, He shut them up with His answer. Jesus has given you permission, credentials, and the authority to carry out life as He designed it. What is stopping you?

As leaders, are we the ones who are using our positions to "lord it over" others? Or, are we sending them out with full permission, credentials, and authority from Christ? Touchy subject. Too much of the time we have not given them permission to do anything except what we want. I can say this because I have been part of the problem in the past. No more!

HOW TO HAND OFF

Do you think it is possible to get those over 45 to sit down with those below 35 and talk about God, life, the world, and their views, without thinking they have an agenda? I think it is. How to do that? Just do it. Get some of your good leaders who are over 45 and love Jesus and get some leaders and potential leaders under 35 who love Jesus. Get them to start talking. You don't necessarily need to decide something. So, no voting allowed. Just get them to start talking and genuinely listening to each other for the purpose of understanding each other. Pick a monthly place and time that is neutral, have some coffee and cookies and a few questions. See what God can do. Let ideas flow. Ask some of the questions throughout the chapters that are nonthreatening. No finger pointing.

I think it is important that you have people who genuinely love Jesus, not the church system. If you have too many who love the system more than they love Jesus, they will fight any time it seems that the system is at fault or in jeopardy. If Jesus is the center and the core, then the discussion will be more about Him and the world in which His kingdom on earth exists. Keep the discussion focused on how we interact with people, not how we set up or change systems to create one that works. That can come later.

As leaders, do you hold back permission from your people?

Andy Stanley at the Catalyst Conference in fall '08 asked this question: "How can we get older churches with buildings to work with younger church plants for the whole kingdom?" At least that is how I remember the question. I think I have an answer. The older ones need to loosen their grip on their stuff and the newer plants need to quit thinking they have the market cornered on correct theology and practice. We could start by getting multi-denominational leaders to start dialogue about how to get the churches to cooperate. We could even design an eHarmony-type site for churches that are looking. Both sides. Established churches looking to use their stuff for the kingdom but are not sure how, and the new plants looking for places to meet who have very little funding.

THE OLDER TEACH THE YOUNGER

God tells us in Titus that it is a good idea. Paul even tells Titus how to instruct an older man. So wisdom does flow both ways. Can we find some ways to allow the next generation to make the decisions on HOW we reach the nations? Since so many churches are headed for the cliff, it couldn't hurt. It is going to be theirs soon anyway. Or they will just go start their own. Can we take the discussions started earlier and build some action plans in the HOW-WHERE-WHEN areas which fuel the fires of those above 45 as well as those below 45?

And, for those in the next generation, can you allow yourself to be part of the bigger picture and not a subplot which blows past everyone? Can you see the value of generational interaction with the established churches and help them redeem what they have?

It doesn't matter who you are or how old you are. Hold a bit less tightly what you have been given...loosen your grip! Let's all hand Him to the world together.

JESUS GOES VIRAL

We use the term viral a lot when it comes to YouTube. Susan Boyle (the *Britain's Got Talent* sensation) got over 12 million hits in less than a few days. That is viral. That is Christ's intent. If He is in you, and you are mobile, then He could go viral. Go back and look at the tubes in chapter five again. If you have ANY connection with others, He should be your number one contagion. The problem is... He is not. Duty, obligation, and ritual seem to have been the rule of the day. We have been taught the wrong things, and we have kept Him cubed up!

Release Him on the planet. Be a part of ReleasingChurches. org.

DISCUSSION GROUP

How can you be a part of Jesus going viral? Isn't that what it really is all about anyway? His love flowing through us into the lives of others in such a way that they know Him better and are changed to look more like Him each day. Then worship him because and in the midst of all that. Are you ready?

You will not see this same paragraph at the end of any other chapter. Now Go and reSymbol the church.

About the Author

DOUG IS CURRENTLY THE Pastor of New Venues at First Baptist Church, Orlando, Florida. He starts video venues and researches church adoption possibilities.

In prior years, he was the Adult Development Pastor at First Orlando—overseeing all aspects of the educational ministry for the 3,500+ in Sunday School as well as men's, women's, and recreation ministry. It was a great job, but just didn't fit who God was making him to be for the future.

Most recently he started a nonprofit group called ReleasingChurches.org, which is designed to help "good churches get better." RC is currently consulting with three megachurches. Many times he has to ask the Dr. Phil question, "So, how is that working for you?"

He has two other books in progress. One is with David Ferguson of GreatCommandment.net called *The Fellowship God Longs For*. Another, entitled *Stable Chaos*, will help people to walk through instability on purpose directly toward God.

He loves coming up with new ways of explaining God and His ways to people who care. Most of all he wants to help those who follow Jesus to become who He sees them to be while they disciple others as He did.